WITNESS
TO
WATER

WITNESS TO WATER

One Photographer's Mission to Defend
THE COLORADO RIVER

PETE McBRIDE

Hierophant publishing

Copyright © 2026 by Pete McBride

All rights reserved, including the right to reproduce this work in any form whatsoever, without permission in writing from the publisher, except for brief passages in connection with a review.

Cover design by Adrian Morgan
Cover photo © Pete McBride
Interior photos © Pete McBride
Grand Canyon map © Pete McBride
Ganges River basin map by Rainer Lesniewski | Shutterstock
Colorado River basin, Gila River, and Yampa River
maps courtesy of Westcliff Publishing
Print book interior design by Frame25 Productions

Hierophant Publishing
San Antonio, TX
www.hierophantpublishing.com

If you are unable to order this book from your local bookseller, you may order directly from the publisher.

Library of Congress Control Number has been applied for.

ISBN: 978-1-950253-51-7

10 9 8 7 6 5 4 3 2 1

To my family who ground me
My parents who gave me wings
And to Heidi for steering me home

Contents

Foreword   ix

Introduction   1

1. Chasing Water   11

2. Sacred and Scarce   41

3. Delta Dawn   59

4. River Dance   77

5. The Call of the Canyon   93

6. A Canyon in the Crosshairs   107

7. A Voice for Rivers   139

8. The Wrong Kind of Quiet   151

9. Shifting Course   161

10. What Rises from the Depths   175

Conclusion   197

Afterword   207

Acknowledgments   211

Foreword

If rivers are poems, as those among us who love them deeply believe they are, then the story of what the Colorado River once was—and what it will never be again—is perhaps best understood as both a Homerian epic and a Shakespearean tragedy.

The first stanza of the Colorado's ancient odyssey opens humbly and without fanfare, as many great stories do: in this case with a silver stream threading across a fern-draped meadow deep in the heart of what is now Rocky Mountain National Park. For more than six million years it tumbled through the fir and pine forests of the Never Summer Mountains while gathering up the runoff of half a dozen cold-water creeks and rivers cascading from the tops of the Rockies—the Fraser, the Blue, the Eagle, the Roaring Fork, the Crystal, and the Gunnison—while cutting a diagonal slant down the western slope of Colorado and then Utah.

From there, the river wheeled south, drilling through an all-but-impenetrable labyrinth of lonely terraces and soaring cliffs until, somewhere out in that wind-raked ocean of rock, deep inside today's Canyonlands National Park, it was joined by its longest tributary, the Green River, which came all the way down from the mountains of Wyoming, almost doubling the Colorado's flow.

Moving south into Arizona, the water turned west to cut across the Kaibab Plateau, then south again, making a beeline along the California border and into Mexico, where the river spread across more than two million acres of delta that was once one of the greatest desert estuaries on earth—a watery republic populated by egrets and cormorants, avocets and mallards, wigeon and teal, as well as countless bobcats, coyotes, raccoons, and deer—before delivering itself into the Sea of Cortez.

All told, the water ran for 1,450 miles, and in the course of that journey the ancestral Colorado—which is to say the river that flowed across the Southwest prior to the era when white Europeans settlers established a foothold during the nineteenth century—behaved unlike any other river, anywhere.

In the thousand miles downstream from its headwaters, the river and its tributaries excavated seventeen major chasms, the last of which, the Grand Canyon, stands as the most magnificent of them all: an open-aired cathedral featuring mile-high walls and a dozen layers of rock whose bloodlines reach more than 1.7 billion years into the past, a tapestry of deep time encompassing one-third the lifespan of our planet and roughly a tenth of the age of the universe itself.

Starting in the spring of 1931 with the construction of the Hoover Dam, we raised nineteen large dams and reservoirs along the Colorado and its tributaries, a sequence of projects that transformed the wildest river in the West to what it is today: something that more closely resembles a municipal waterworks system than a river—a network of pipes and valves, faucets and catchment tubs that basically function as plumbing.

Every cubic foot of the Colorado's flow is gauged and metered and accounted for, and the timing and volume of each discharge through every set of penstocks and turbines is calibrated to optimize electricity generation and maximize power revenue. Nothing happens on the river that has not been carefully planned, reviewed, and approved. And for good reason, because the Colorado is now the lifeblood of the entire Southwest, a resource upon which forty million citizens spread across a dozen major cities and towns plus 5.5 million acres of farmland are completely and totally dependent.

No river in the western hemisphere is more rigorously controlled, more stringently regulated, or more heavily litigated than the Colorado. And none has been exploited so ruthlessly. According to one set of calculations, every drop of water the river contains is used and reused up to seventeen times before the river itself dries up and dies in the Sonoran Desert south of the border. In all but the very wettest years, not so much as a teaspoon of the Colorado River reaches the sea.

In addition to all these distinctions, the Colorado has one other superlative: it is one of the world's most documented rivers, especially within the Grand Canyon. And among all the storytellers who have strived to capture this river's moods, its power, its cadences, its vulnerability, and the paramount importance it holds for every person who lives along its banks or is sustained by its waters, none, to the best of my knowledge, has a longer, deeper, or more passionate relationship with the Colorado than Pete McBride.

I've seen this firsthand during the many years we've worked together. I've watched him document each section of the river, in all seasons, under every condition imaginable. During our end-to-end Grand Canyon traverse, a journey that took more than a year to complete, the challenges of creating a portrait of a landscape as hostile as it was beautiful often turned an immense challenge into a nightmare. But from the first blush of dawn to the star-draped immensity of the night, Pete's love for the Colorado only seemed to grow with time.

This book is about my friend's obsession with a river that offers up a reminder of what we know to be true, but too often choose to forget: that we live by the grace and at the mercy of forces greater than ourselves, which work on a scale of space and time we cannot begin to imagine. But aside from stepping into a boat and heading off downstream, there's no better vessel for contemplating this truth than the book that you hold in your hands—my best friend's lifelong journey along the greatest river in the American Southwest.

—Kevin Fedarko
New York Times best-selling author of *A Walk in the Park*

Introduction

> To stick your hands into the river is to feel the
> cords that bind the earth together in one piece.
> —Barry Holstun Lopez, *River Notes: The Dance of Herons*

Under a cloudless Sonoran sky, I paddle my craft downstream into unknown waters in a forgotten estuary. I am a few miles into Mexico, just south of the US border. I've passed beneath the last highway bridge and am gazing into the soft January light. In the flat expanse ahead, shrouded in the distance by a barren mountain range, sits the famed Colorado River delta—once known as the most extensive riparian corridor in the American Southwest.

I am paddling a small, inflatable packraft with my food, fresh drinking water, camping gear, emergency supplies, and cameras all tucked inside dry bags in a big backpack jammed into the bow at my feet.

The shallow flow of water turns left into a cluster of dense, dark green tamarisk bushes, a thirsty invasive shrub that has rooted itself throughout the area. Two paddle strokes later, I notice the water change. Its tannin-colored flow has disappeared. A dark chocolaty, grainy foam surrounds my craft and starts to grow as if I've woken up some ancient alien quicksand beast. I glide a few more feet, my paddle now striking bottom, and the foam swallows up even more of my tiny boat. Then my packraft hits bottom and screeches to a stop. I'm stuck in this stew-like foam, surrounded by plastic bottles, inky brown scum, chunks of green ooze, and who knows what else.

I look at my friend Jon, our faces registering disbelief.

I didn't expect this paddling trip down the Colorado River to end in a pit of muck. We are nearly a hundred miles from the ocean and there is no more water ahead, only a bed of sand and cracked earth. The river hasn't just dried up—it's perished before my eyes, miles upon miles before it kisses the sea.

~

Before taking this *National Geographic* assignment to accompany my friend Jon Waterman on his source-to-sea Colorado River mission, I'd worked as a photographer in over seventy-five countries on seven continents. I focused on expeditions and remote adventures and prided myself on getting up close and personal no matter where I was—using my camera as a passport to tell other people's stories.

As a result, many of the assignments I took presented unique challenges, to put it lightly. On my first assignment, the antique replica World War I biplane I was flying in was intercepted by fighter jets. On another job reporting on the narcotics trade, I was held at gunpoint by a thirteen-year-old and later deported from the Horn of Africa. That particularly ulcer-inducing incident scared me enough that I chose to focus my lenses away from human conflict and toward the wild, natural wonders of our world.

In Nepal, I stared down an avalanche at twenty thousand feet on the flanks of Mount Everest and decided that, since there was no way to escape it, I might as well snap some photos. With death seemingly imminent, I figured my family and friends might like to know what happened to me if they ever found my camera.

I kayaked along the coast of Antarctica and decided to scuba dive alone, under the ice. Unwise, perhaps, but it was breathtaking—literally. Another time, a rhino in Malawi charged me while I was documenting conservationists attempting to thwart wildlife poachers with GPS beacons. To evade this leathery explosion of muscle and speed, I chose to scale an acacia tree, grasping thorns with my bare hands. Luckily, my camera was more or less spared.

And then there was my trip to the Arctic, when I swam in 37-degree water with a pod of orca. One male pinged me with sonar, nearly jolting my heart from my body—not the best feeling for a journalist with heart issues. He later swept his pectoral fin over my head and blew bubbles in my face, as if playfully reminding me who was boss.

Other assignments brought more awe and wonder but took their pound of flesh in the form of stitches, broken bones, scorpion bites, severe dehydration, meningitis, dysentery, and more. Experiences like those etched themselves into my memory, but nothing shook me to the core quite like feeling my packraft scrape bottom as the mighty Colorado River turned into what I now refer to as the frothy Frappuccino pit of sludge, sewage, and river demise.

I'm not sure why this moment moved my soul so profoundly. I suspect that, for me, this wasn't just another hard-fought assignment—and it wasn't just any river: This was a story about

Jon Waterman's packraft runs aground at the polluted end of the Colorado River.

the western lifeline that was born in the snowcapped peaks of my childhood home, the Rocky Mountains of Colorado. Some have called the Colorado River the most loved and litigated body of water in the world. Others have dubbed it an economic engine, a ribbon of life, and even "the American Nile."

But for me, it's just my backyard river.

At the moment when the polluted foam nearly swallowed me whole and the river's flow ran dry before my eyes, the story became personal—and it changed the course of my life.

This is a story decades in the making about a threatened river I love and a resource none of us can live without: fresh water.

~

A friend once told me that the Colorado River today is merely a western plumbing system. I nodded as if I understood, but I didn't. When I was a kid, I loved fishing from the Colorado's banks and canoeing its whiskey-colored flows, marveling at the quiet power hidden beneath the surface's lazy appearance. Later I would hone my swimming skills in those sneaky-fast waters. After working in the hot western Colorado sun with my brother, loading hay by hand, we would jump in to wash the dust off. No matter how hard we stroked and kicked, we got flushed hundreds of yards downstream. How could my friend compare this wet and wonderful ecosystem to an inert collection of pipes?

But the Colorado River isn't just my childhood playground. It's the lifeblood of the American Southwest, a 1,450-mile artery that begins in the Rocky Mountains of Colorado and historically emptied into the Gulf of California in Mexico. Today, this mighty river supports approximately forty million people across seven US states—Colorado, Wyoming, Utah, New Mexico, Nevada, Arizona, and California—and two Mexican states—Baja California and Sonora. According to the Lincoln Institute of Land Policy, as of 2019, its waters irrigated about five million acres of US farmland, growing a whopping 15 percent of America's produce and 13 percent of its livestock. Every winter, when you bite into a crisp green leaf of baby spinach or a juicy red strawberry, you're most likely consuming Colorado River water. Seventy percent of the water in Lower Basin states goes to alfalfa production, with some farms producing over twelve cuttings a year—much of it exported to places like Saudi Arabia and China.

The river also generates hydroelectric power through massive infrastructure projects like the Hoover Dam and the Glen Canyon Dam, creating energy for millions of homes and businesses, and supports tourism, rafting, and fishing industries worth billions of dollars.

Yet for decades now, we've known that the water in the Colorado River is over-allocated—every drop of it assigned to some human purpose, with nothing left over for the plants and animals that depend on it, let alone for its own right to exist. We've been so eager to use the river water to grow our food and power our industries that we've forgotten that a river, too, needs water to thrive. While we water fields and fountains and make suburbs bloom in the desert, the river itself has been suffering.

This, I learned, is what we are doing to the Colorado River: assigning it the impossible task of delivering more water than it actually holds, while leaving nothing for it to sustain itself. For decades, we have been asking the river to defy the laws of physics, while ignoring the increasingly dire consequences for people, animals, and plant life downstream. Now, the river is dying—with catastrophic consequences for all of us.

The Colorado River is managed under a system known as the "Law of the River"—which is plagued by a very simple math problem. There are decades of treaties and court decisions layered on top of the original Colorado River Compact of 1922, but in essence, the Law of the River divides the Colorado River into two basins—the Upper Basin (Colorado, Wyoming, Utah, and New Mexico) and the Lower Basin (Arizona, Nevada, and California). Each basin gets 50 percent of the average flow—7.5 million acre-feet of water, totaling 15 million acre-feet. Mexico was later granted its own allotment of 1.5 million acre-feet. You can visualize an acre-foot as a football field covered with a layer of water one foot deep.

The problem is that the river doesn't carry 16.5 million acre-feet of water anymore—not even close. These days, it's flowing at about 20 percent less than historical averages. It's like we used to have a large drink—and equally large straws to quench our supersized thirst. Today, this Western soda fountain only serves medium-sized drinks—but our supersized thirst and straws remain, sipping to the very last drop.

Now, climate change has led to lackluster snowpack in the Rockies, which means the river's flow is trending smaller. Thirsty plants suck up more of the spring runoff before it can reach the river, and the sun's relentless rays cause massive evaporation from human-created reservoirs and canals. Meanwhile, the Southwestern US is experiencing a thousand-year megadrought, putting extra pressure on an already stressed system.

These challenges aren't unique to the Colorado. Rivers worldwide face similar pressures from overuse, pollution, and climate change. From the Nile to the Ganges to the Amazon, we are seeing rivers falter under the weight of our demands on them. The Colorado serves as a microcosm of our fraught relationship with nature and our most precious and increasingly scarce resource—fresh water.

≈

It was my father who pitched me on the idea of photographing the Colorado from its tributary headwaters in our greater backyard of the Elk Mountains to its historic end point at the Gulf of California. At the time, I was in my late thirties and had been working as an adventure photographer for more than a decade. After getting my start at *High Country News* in Colorado, I'd traveled all over the world on assignment for magazines like *National Geographic*, *Smithsonian*, and *Outside*. This was back in the day when glossy print magazines still existed and had assignment budgets. Today, such publications have dwindled or vanished as online media has blossomed.

I was a rolling stone and a bit of an adrenaline junkie, tumbling from one risky assignment to the next with little time to put down roots, but collecting stories and forging friendships made me feel alive. I'd also started to develop a deep interest in water—that limited natural resource that often resides somewhere at the heart of most stories.

In the midst of it all, my parents started lovingly ribbing me about if I would ever settle down and start a family. They never failed to remind me that my older brother Johno also had an adventurous life coaching the US Ski Team, but still found time to get married and have a family. My sister Kate competed as a professional ski racer, ran a small raw-milk dairy, earned a degree as a vet tech, and also became a dedicated mother. Surely I could learn something from their example. But at the time I couldn't even keep my houseplants alive, let alone a relationship.

One October between assignments, my father invited me to join him on a flight—ostensibly to "look for missing cows" hiding in brushy backcountry. But once we took off, his voice came crackling through my headset.

"Why don't you do a project here?" he asked. "From the air, you can see how damn dry it's getting. Why don't you do a project on water?"

I glanced at him and raised my eyebrows. But he was right. It was time I did a project closer to home. Initially, I think my father pitched the idea as a sneaky way to lure me back to Colorado to settle down. But like many people, he'd also noticed that the snowpack above our land was changing. In the winter, the snow was falling later and melting sooner. The runoff flowed more unpredictably, lurching between droughts and flash floods. The Center for Snow and Avalanche Studies in Silverton, Colorado, had discovered that desert dust was blowing all the way from the Southwest and coating Colorado's mountains, which made the snow absorb more heat from the sun and melt up to six weeks earlier than it otherwise would. People seemed to be experiencing collective amnesia, as our definition of a "good ski year" began to look like what we would have called a thin ski year just a decade before.

I couldn't have known then how my dad's suggestion would transform my life and send me on a twenty-year journey to witness and document a river in peril. After years of documenting the stories of others around the world, this book is the story of my journey: what I saw when I followed our water down my greater backyard river from the mountains to the sea, and what I learned about the fragility of the natural systems we too often take for granted. It's a story about what happens when we ask too much, and what happens when we start to pay attention: to our rivers, to our landscapes, and to the people who call us home.

Chapter 1

Chasing Water

"Shape up, hurry up." My dad prodded me as we prepared for our first flight. "You know this plane costs $300 an hour to fly, and you are dinking around!"

It was spring of 2008, and I had struck a deal with my dad. I'd landed an assignment about the Colorado, and I needed aerial photographs, so I hired him to fly me around in his single-engine Cessna 180, a bush plane sometimes referred to as the "pickup truck of the sky" for its ruggedness and versatility. Its high-wing configuration gave it great downward visibility—a boon for a photographer like me. Dad's was white, with a red stripe down the fuselage and purple wings. For years, he'd used it to fly mountain rescue missions, a few business trips, and some pleasure flights thrown in for good measure. And yes, in the fall, he sometimes used it to search for lost cows.

For this project, I told him that I'd reimburse him for fuel and maintenance, and he agreed he would donate his time and bush-pilot skills.

"Yeah, yeah, yeah, I'm coming," I shot back, checking to make sure I'd brought extra batteries and cards for my cameras. "I'm just getting my gear ready."

Taking off from his bumpy grass strip at 7,900 feet, we rose up over the high mountain cattle ranch my parents had bought in 1979. I watched as the old ranch house my father designed and its hand-built outbuildings shrank down to the size of toys, along with the flat-roofed building that served as hangar and garage for a 1970s Land Cruiser and an ATV, the irrigation pond we swam in, and my mom's garden, with its border of old bed frames painted bright blue. Every part of it was as familiar to me as the blood running through my veins: so close I barely realized it was there.

My parents were adventurous types, drawn to the Aspen area for its skiing and scenery. My dad liked to say that the people who moved to Aspen back then were the black sheep of their families—the ones who broke away to do something different. As he put it, "If you loved the mountains, loved the skiing, and had a sense of humor, you were in." He described Aspen in the 1960s as a college campus for adults. Most people had a job doing something or other, but they never let work get in the way of a good time.

Although he wasn't exactly a black sheep, Dad had found his way to Aspen after getting disillusioned with corporate life. He'd gone to Princeton, where he made hockey-team history by scoring the most points in a season—a record that stood for five decades. Later, his hockey talent earned him a spot on the US national team, where he scored the only goal in a game against Russia that ended in an embarrassing loss of 10–1.

Eager for new challenges, he signed up for a stint in the military with the Air National Guard, and took his first "real" job selling fiberglass for Owens-Corning in San Francisco, where he met my mom, Laurie—who everyone calls Moutie. When she moved to New York City to teach, he feared he would lose her to her many other suitors—so he surprised her by showing up unannounced, and soon they were engaged.

By that point, my dad had realized that there was no *way* he was going to pursue the Chicago finance career his father had hoped he would—commuting by train, cocktails at 4:00 p.m., golfing on the weekends. His job sent him to Denver, and he started hearing rumors of excellent skiing in Vail, which at the time was little more than a dot on the map—far from the fancy resort town it is today. Enamored by the place, he quit his job, used his savings to build a two-room cabin himself, and brought my mother there to start their new life.

Luckily for him, my mom was up for anything as long as there was fun to be had, friends to be made, music, and adventure. A Stanford-educated tennis star, pianist, painter, and schoolteacher, she loved animals and was excited about the prospect of living in a place with bears, mountain lions, elk, and other wildlife—not to mention a place where she could let her wild spirit run free, far from her urban upbringing. She relished Colorado's four seasons, the gardens she could grow in the summer, and the mountains she could explore year-round and ski in the winter.

At the time, the population of Vail was only around fifty people, many of them living in cabins and shacks they built themselves. There was a feeling of excitement in the air—of young people making their own rules, building their vision on uncharted territory, and coming up with creative ways to pay the bills. There were sleigh rides, Fourth of July parties, treasure hunts, and rafting trips. People knew each other and watched each other's kids. My older brother was born, and soon, my older sister came along. My dad undertook a number of construction projects to support his growing family, including a clock tower that remains an iconic landmark to this day.

In 1966, a developer named Bill Janss who'd noticed my dad's work in Vail recruited him to help line up tenants and work on the design for the commercial square in Snowmass, a new town and ski area about a hundred miles southeast of Vail. The opportunity was too good to pass up, so my parents moved to Aspen, where they rented a four-bedroom house downtown for $200 a month. There, they would soon cultivate new friends and community with people like Walter and Elizabeth Paepke, who founded the Aspen Institute, and Fritz and Fabi Benedict, a couple so influential in preserving open space that they eventually had backcountry huts named in their honor.

My mother likes to boast now that when she was pregnant with my sister, she beat Stein Eriksen, the famous alpine ski racer and Olympic gold medalist, in a tennis match. In those early days, she says, people were more interested in what you did than who you were.

I entered the scene in 1971. When I was nine years old, my parents sold our home and used the proceeds to buy what is now our family home in Old Snowmass, an unincorporated community about twenty miles from town. My parents' friends thought they'd lost it—who uproots to the middle of nowhere with three kids in tow? How would we get to school? What about friends? *Have you lost your marbles?*

In joking deference to these concerns, that became the name of our new home: Lost Marbles Ranch.

Although neither of my parents had any experience with livestock beyond some chickens and goats, they got advice from an old-timer who lived nearby, and we soon had a herd of cattle. They also took on a pair of sturdy and seemingly tireless Percheron horses named Teddy and Charlie that we used to pull a hay sled to feed our cattle in the winter months. Year-round, the ranch was home to an astonishing array of wildlife: elk, black bears, badgers, and beavers splashing in the creeks and relentlessly damming our irrigation ditches or eating my mother's trees. In the spring, you could hear chickadees, mountain bluebirds, and other songbirds trilling all around, and a carpet of lupine, larkspur, columbine, and wild iris would spring up in pockets in the hay meadows.

As a kid, I did not love the logistics of living so far in the country. Sometimes it felt like I spent my whole life in transit—falling asleep on the bus on the long ride to school, missing my bus, getting rides home from sports practice with teachers or the parents of friends. After realizing Aspen lacked a youth hockey league, my dad founded one just after I was born. My siblings and I spent so much time at the skating rink in town it would have been easier to throw down a sleeping bag and live there rather than endure the long drives back and forth.

My dad was a good hockey coach, but he was also stern, especially with his own sons. He would rarely compliment our playing. Instead, he would push us harder. I remember him hollering at me when I lost the puck or forgot to keep my head up.

"Where were you on that pass?" he'd shout. "Get lower on that puck, Pete! I said *low!*"

I remember one practice where I got crunched in the boards and snapped my thumb back. It hurt like hell, but my dad was short on sympathy.

"Aw, stop whining," he said. "Skate it off. You'll be fine."

After practice, he took me to the local hospital, where an X-ray revealed that my thumb was fractured. On the car ride home, I confronted him about why he was always so tough on me in front of the team.

"My thumb is *broken*," I said. "But you acted like I was being a baby."

I was quivering with indignation. He patted my arm.

"Oh Pete," he said. "I need to be harder on you than any of the other players because I'm your dad. Otherwise people will say, 'Oh, he's the coach's son, he gets special treatment.' I want you to get credit for your hard work, but it can't look like it's coming from me. It needs to come from your teammates."

I was glad that I'd confronted him, and that he'd told me. From that point on, I knew that when he was yelling at me from the bench or on the ice, it was partly for show. Still, it didn't make everything easy. We'd get home from hockey practice at 10:00 p.m., after making the long, often slow winter drive home, and I'd struggle to be up at 6:00 a.m. to catch the school bus. I was growing, so all I wanted to do was sleep. Often, I felt envious of my friends who could walk or bike to each other's houses and catch an hour of extra sleep before school.

Aside from these logistical hassles, the ranch was a magical place for a dreamy, introspective kid like me. Doing my chores, feeding orphaned calves, or collecting eggs, I would study things at length. When sports didn't interfere, I'd draw and later paint. I loved showing my mom the drawings or paintings I'd worked on for hours, and seeing her hang them in her art studio with her own watercolors. Surrounded by open space, with no sounds except those of nature, I could let my mind roam. When you spend that much time gazing at your surroundings, you see things other people don't: the way a sudden gust of wind ripples across the surface of a pond, or how the mountains glow purple after the sun has set. Without realizing it, I was already developing my eye as a photographer.

Living on a ranch, there was always work to do. In the summers, I spent mornings "chasing water": moving portable dams and linking aluminum pipes to gravity-fed sprinklers. Our irrigation water came from the fourteen-thousand-foot peaks to the south of our valley. Snowmelt fed these mountain creeks, and we would divert a portion into old ditches, pour it across our fields, and use it to grow hay to feed our cattle.

Each August, I spent long hours cutting that hay. I'd sit high above the field in the swather (a twelve-foot-wide hay mower), staring at the results of the summer's work. I often thought about water, wondering how much went into the field and how much returned to the creek.

Now, as my dad and I climbed up to nearly fifteen thousand feet, I could see our creek flowing north to the Roaring Fork River, then merging with it and turning west. Thirty miles later, it would pour into the Colorado and begin its journey to Mexico.

I turned to my dad.

"You doing okay this high?" I asked. "Should we use the oxygen tube? I don't want you getting sleepy at this altitude."

"Pfft," he said. "I've been flying planes since before you were even a *thought*. I'll be fine. You're the sleepy one. . . . I could do this with my eyes closed." He pretended to fly with his eyes closed for a few seconds. We both laughed into the headset.

My father wasn't exaggerating. He'd earned his pilot's license at fourteen. When I added up the decades he'd been pilot in command, it was longer than I'd been alive. I knew I was in good hands.

"Wow, look at those second homes," he said, spotting what looked like castles, with multicar garages, outbuildings, pools, and sprawling green lawns.

"Bank right, let me take a look," I said. He turned the yoke to the right, added some right rudder pedal, and we circled at 45-degree bank angles.

My dad groaned. "When you were a kid, there were average homes and small ski bum cabins. Nearly everyone here was a full-time resident—teachers, architects, builders, doctors, artists," he said. "The amount of energy it takes to keep these second homes going while they sit empty . . . the amount of *water* it takes to keep those lawns green. . . ." He trailed off.

I'd heard this kind of gripe from him many times before. "When are you going to join them to carve the ranch up into a shopping plaza, motocross track, and resort?" I teased.

"Ha . . . over my dead body," he said.

~

Earlier that spring, I'd traveled to the Colorado River's headwaters in Rocky Mountain National Park. There, I'd joined my friend Jon Waterman, a writer and fellow Coloradan who was also curious about the river. Jon had made a name for himself by making a 2,200-mile journey through the Northwest Passage, braving frigid waters and encounters with polar bears to document life in the Arctic. For our project, Jon would paddle the entire Colorado River—a distance of 1,450 miles—while I would photograph the journey from a few different perspectives: paddling next to Jon in a tiny inflatable packraft, flying in small aircrafts to include a bird's-eye perspective, and doing plenty of bushwhacking. All in all, the project would take five months to complete.

Standing next to Jon at La Poudre Pass with a snowbank melting nearby, I found myself staring at the birthplace of America's most iconic river. This small and unassuming seep of water, carving out a channel through some spongy alpine grass, was the headwaters of the Colorado. As I photographed the spot, I felt like I was meeting a long-lost benefactor. I thought of all the childhood memories that were tied to this water—swimming, water-skiing, fishing, even skiing on its snowpack—and of all the ways the river had quietly supported aspects of my life I often took for granted, from irrigating the farms that grew my food to turning the turbines whose electricity charged the batteries in my camera. I felt an unexpected prickle of gratitude, responsibility, and connection.

For the next few days, Jon and I paddled together where the river isn't much wider than one of the irrigation ditches on our family ranch. It was a peak water weekend, and snowmelt in the high country made for a lively flow, even as much of the water was already being diverted to the Grand Ditch—a fourteen-mile-long diversion project that takes water from the Colorado River headwaters to the dry eastern plains. This is the first of roughly two dozen major transbasin diversions that reroute water from the Colorado River basin over the Continental Divide to the eastern slope.

The Colorado River watershed is an intricate network of rivers and streams encompassing most of the American southwest and part of northwest Mexico.

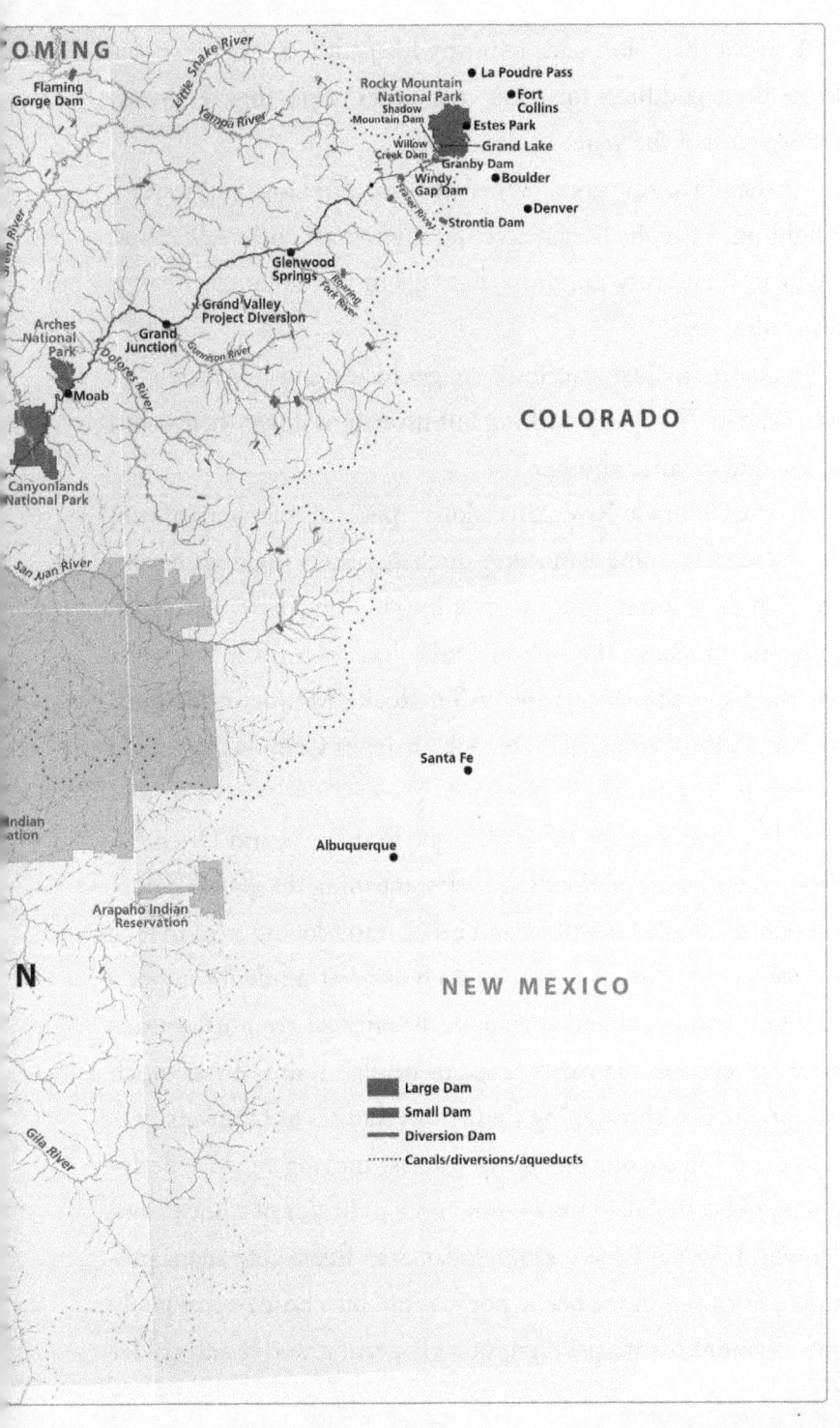

"Look at that," Jon said, pointing his paddle at the diversion. "We've been paddling for what, ten miles? And they're already sucking out half the water in the river."

"As the old saying goes, 'Whiskey is for drinking, and water is for fighting,'" I replied, maneuvering my raft around a fallen tree. "I've heard that every raindrop that falls in the Colorado River is already allocated."

Jon snorted. "Just wait until we get to the end in Mexico . . . *if* we make it. The river's nothing but diversions down there—just one canal maze after another."

On the Colorado River, diversions consist of a network of tunnels and canals, some hand-dug ditches, others lined with concrete, that draw water from the river into holding reservoirs, cities, farms, and ranches. The Grand Ditch has been diverting water from the Colorado since 1890. After Rocky Mountain National Park was established in 1915, it took an act of Congress to extend the ditch to its final length in 1936.

Today, advocates for the park argue that the Grand Ditch has interfered with natural flooding cycles, meaning there's less damp, fertile soil available for willow and other water-loving trees to take root. Meanwhile, invasive species such as great mullein can get a foothold in drier soil and spread. A diminished river also means that water levels in the park's precious peatlands drop by as much as twenty inches, threatening these powerhouses of biodiversity.

Jon and I made our way down the fast-moving streams, dodging piles of beetle-killed trees—one more indicator of a hotter and drier world. When I was a kid, regular deep freeze cold snaps prevented explosions in the beetle population, but those freezes rarely come anymore. As we paddled, quickly getting wetter and colder with icy splashes seeping past the spray skirts on our packrafts, I thought about how little freedom this river got to enjoy before it was harnessed and put to work. The Colorado River had hardly sprung out of its headwaters and already we were diverting it miles from its natural course to water our fields and power our cities. We were mere hours into our journey down one of the longest and mightiest rivers in America, and the wildest part of the river was already behind us.

Seeing the Colorado through fresh eyes awakened something urgent in me. Every bend of the river was revealing something new about the ways that humans were transforming a six-million-year-old force of nature into the highly engineered plumbing system it is today.

Jon is twenty-one years older than me. Just before we'd met up at La Poudre Pass, he'd scattered his mother's ashes near the river's headwaters. She had died just one month before the start of our expedition, following a lengthy battle with cancer. I knew that our journey down the Colorado had taken on extra meaning for him as a result.

At thirty-seven, I was still under the impression that my parents were invincible. Sure, my dad was looking a little skinny relative to the buff hockey player he'd been in his prime, but he still coached and played hockey, and both my parents skied like the wind. My mother, a breast cancer survivor, could still beat me in Ping-Pong. I often joked that when they removed her breast, it made her even faster.

There were both as sharp and witty as they'd ever been. Sure, they wanted me closer to home, but I still had plenty of time.

"Get to know them while you still can," Jon told me that night while we were heating up our food over the camp stove. "It's just like this river—you think the water will last forever, and it's too easy to ignore the signs when it's running out."

～

The next day, Jon and I left Rocky Mountain National Park and followed the stream as it wound its way through private ranchlands. Here, we encountered a whole new type of hazard: barbed-wire fences strung across the river, just waiting to puncture our inflatable rafts. At one point, Jon's raft ran into a fencepost just as I was trying to guide mine between two strands of wire; my raft flipped backward, sweeping me under the icy water. As Jon scrambled for my lost paddle, I swam under the barbed wire and made my way to the riverbank to regroup, thankful that my camera was safely wrapped up in a drybag.

After checking to make sure that my raft hadn't gotten punctured, we carried on. The blue spruce and occasional aspen or cottonwood trees gave way to hay fields, cows, and a gravel pit. All around, we could see creeks and washes swollen with snowmelt rushing off the mountainsides and feeding into the stream. Before we knew it, the unassuming ditch we'd started paddling in had become a raging torrent. The day before, three boaters had drowned while attempting to navigate this kind of treacherous water.

"I don't like this," Jon shouted. I knew he was thinking about his wife and kids, imagining how it would be for them if he took a stupid risk and got hurt.

"Me neither," I replied. "Let's get outta here."

We pulled our packrafts out of the river, deflated them, and called it a day.

~

Now nearly out of the high country, I left Jon to paddle the next stretch without me. As great as it was to experience the river by packraft, it was impossible to shoot images. Every time I saw something I wanted to photograph, I had to pull my camera from a drybag and paddle the boat with one arm—not an easy task. Often, by the time I got ready, the image I was trying to make was gone as I'd moved downstream. One afternoon I got lucky and got a photo of Jon paddling by a young moose, but quickly found myself tangled in a fallen tree soon after. Paddling on the river limited me to a close-up perspective. I craved a better vantage, too; a bird's-eye view of the river's twists and turns, and the many ways it was being used by human beings on a larger scale.

For this, I needed a pilot—a good one, and one who might cut me a deal. Luckily, I knew just the man for the job. What better way to stay closer to home and get some quality time with my dad than enlist his help for this project?

~

Now, my dad pointed out the cockpit window at a sunny mountain slope. "Look at *that*! No snow left at all. You wouldn't have seen that ten years ago."

"Can you bank the plane back around?" I asked. "I want to get a shot."

When the weather allowed, we flew sections of the river nearest to the ranch. Right away, I started to see just how many straws were drinking from the river. The state of Colorado has a dilemma: 80 percent of the water lands on the western mountains, but 80 percent of the people live on the eastern plains. From the air, I could see water diverted through endless ditches and canals, funneled toward the thirsty east.

But cities like Denver and Colorado Springs aren't the only things sticking drinking straws into the Colorado River. At the top of Fremont Pass, up to forty thousand acre-feet of water flows into or around the Climax molybdenum mine's treatment ponds. Seen from the sky, these treatment ponds are otherworldly hues of vermillion and burnt sienna due to the dissolved iron, copper, and other metals in the water. Although we may not be used to thinking of mining as a water-intensive activity, this one mine alone uses 7 percent of Denver's water.

My dad and I also flew over miles of range and agricultural lands that looked a lot like our own. Upper Basin ranches like ours only irrigate during summer months, consuming less water than farms in hotter, drier, Lower Basin states that irrigate year-round. Still, water rights are never far from anyone's mind. Every raindrop and snowflake is spoken for before it even hits the ground. In fact, until just a few years ago, it was illegal in Colorado to harvest rainwater from your own downspouts. Those drops were already accounted for by someone else, downstream somewhere in what is already an overallocated system.

On one foray, my father and I flew west, shadowing the river across western Colorado and into the Utah desert. It was fun to act like my father's boss for a change.

"You see those horses back there on the right?" I'd say. "Can you do a quick one-eighty?"

"Aye, aye, captain," he replied. "You know, one of these days, you might have to get a real job."

"Oooh, Pabo boy," I said, pointing my camera down to capture the long, perpendicular shadows the horses cast on the dry ground. "That wouldn't be nearly as fun as this, would it?"

Pete McBride flies over Colorado in his father's Cessna 180, with his father (right) at the controls.

"Maybe. But I'm serious," he said. "Your generation is going to have to fix some of the things my generation broke. All those diversions—the endless sprawl you see around every city, even around the small towns. We thought we were building the future, but we didn't understand what it would cost."

He sighed.

"You know, it didn't used to be this way. Maybe you don't remember it that well, but the river, lakes, reservoirs—they all used to have a *lot* more water—and nobody's talking about it."

~

As the river cuts through the Colorado Plateau, its flow is doubled by the Green River, its largest tributary. Below the confluence, I watched the Colorado enter the first of its desert seas: Lake Powell. Now known as a vacation destination where you can go fishing or Jet-Skiing in a wonderland of glassy water and slick red rocks, Lake Powell was created by flooding a wilderness area called Glen Canyon in 1966.

Our family visited Lake Powell many times when I was a kid, but I didn't realize how big it really was until I saw it from the air. From the cockpit, the reservoir stretched beyond the horizon, a massive blue expanse whose watery arms reached deep into side canyons. It was hard to imagine that underneath all that still blue water, there used to be a living river lushly surrounded by plants and trees.

In its prime, Lake Powell held a whopping 24.3 million acre-feet of water. Today, the lake is shrinking. At the time I flew over with my dad, the West was in its second decade of drought, and everywhere I looked, the 100-foot-high bathtub rings on the lake's edge reminded me how much water we once had.

"Where did it all *go*?" I said.

"Where do you think?" said my dad. "Less snow equals less water. And imagine the evaporation in this heat. We used to be lucky to break ninety once a summer. Now it lingers over ninety for weeks."

We motored toward Page, Arizona, and banked over Glen Canyon Dam. From the air, this 710-foot concrete arching dam looked surprisingly small. But above were flooded oxbows and canyon meanders that reached to the horizon.

"How 'bout it, Pops?" I asked. "Want to fly over the Grand Canyon—and further downstream?"

"Your mother would want to come," he said. After a pause and small adjustment on the fuel mixture he added, "I'd love to, but I'd better get home. You should really find another pilot for that section—someone who knows the flight paths and regulations and can handle the Mojave Desert heat better. But it might be tough for you to find anyone who'll put up with your bossy photo demands." He chuckled into the headset.

"Are you sure?" I asked. "You're doing great."

He just smiled and gave me his hand to shake, as if we were making a pact. "We'll fly again at home when you get back," he said.

≈

It turned out my dad wasn't exactly right about the fountains and lawns in Las Vegas. When I visited the city a few weeks later, I discovered that the truth about its water usage was more nuanced than that. Ninety percent of the water in Las Vegas comes from the Colorado, but its allocation is actually quite small. Vegas hardly existed when the Colorado River Compact divvied up water allotments in 1922, so today the city is forced to use its share wisely.

These days, the city actually pays people to tear out their front lawns. I watched a landscaping crew tear out a lush green lawn in the morning and replace it with desert-friendly shrubs by noon. I asked a Vegas water authority representative how many lawn conversions they'd done, and she told me that since 1999 when the program began, they'd upgraded over two hundred million square feet of turf—saving more than 10 percent of Nevada's Colorado River allocation (about 1.8 percent of the river's annual total water supply). In the years since my visit, they've more than doubled that amount.

A law passed in 2021 prohibits commercial and multifamily properties from watering nonfunctional turf (as opposed to "useful" turf like soccer fields). That same year, the Las Vegas Valley Water District voted to prevent any new golf courses from using water from the Colorado River. Las Vegas has restrictions on swimming pool sizes and car washing, fines for leaks, and laws prohibiting fountains or decorative ponds larger than ten feet. All this has meant that over the past two decades, southern Nevada has added about 750,000 new residents while actually *reducing* its Colorado River water consumption by 31 percent, according to one official.

But not everyone wants to be Vegas. Downstream, the Colorado River becomes the border between Arizona and California, and the straws are abundant. At Lake Havasu, the Colorado River Aqueduct pulls water 242 miles west to Los Angeles. And on the eastern side, the Central Arizona Project (CAP) pumps water 336 miles uphill to Phoenix and Tucson. From the air, those marvels of engineering looked like industrial-sized veins, draining the river's lifeblood and sending it to distant cities to keep them alive.

The 336-mile-long Central Arizona Project carries water uphill to Phoenix, Arizona, and then across the desert to Tuscon, Arizona, where it provides 100 percent of the city's drinking water.

Seen from the air, the scale was truly staggering. Every few miles, I'd see another diversion, another canal, another *demand*. I started to feel a physical ache just from looking at it. How could we do this to the river? Why hadn't we stopped? Wasn't it obvious that we were killing the Colorado?

The ache only intensified below Lake Havasu, when I followed the river south to the Imperial Valley, one of the richest areas of farmland in the United States. Every crop here is entirely fed by Colorado River water.

I realized that I'd never really known this part of the river. It was so different from the one I'd grown up playing in. Whereas the river I knew was rambunctious and alive, what I saw in the Imperial Valley was a river that was confined, fractured, and fading. From my vantage point in the sky, I started seeing the Colorado

River as an orphan, stretched into a maze of concrete canals and a symphony of human thirst.

I couldn't believe I was looking at the same river whose water I'd splashed and played in more than a thousand miles upstream. When the irrigation water on my family's ranch made its way back to the creek and eventually to the Colorado, it ended up here, in this man-made landscape that had more in common with a factory than a wilderness. My entire concept of the Colorado River was changing rapidly. My dad was right: there was a story to be told in my own backyard.

〜

As the river approached Mexico, I reunited with Jon. He'd been paddling for five months by this point, and he had a full beard and looked twenty pounds lighter. His feet were so badly blistered that he could barely walk. I was glad I had decided to do most of the journey by air. Seeing the river from a small plane had opened my eyes to the extent of our demands on its water. Now, however, it was time for me to put my feet on the ground again, and sweat alongside Jon as the river made its way the last hundred miles to the Gulf of California—or tried to, anyway.

For six million years, the Colorado River flowed to the sea. To put this in context, that's more than five and a half million years before modern humans even existed. The river is so much older than us, we're just a blip in its history—and yet in that short time, we have left a profound mark on it.

Historically, the Colorado River terminated in a three-thousand-square-mile estuary in the Gulf of California, also known as the

Sea of Cortez. This vast wetland ecosystem formed as the river deposited sediment at its mouth, creating a seemingly endless network of channels, lagoons, and marshes. This ecologically rich wonderland teemed with jaguars, birds, and cottonwood forests—a sanctuary of biodiversity in the midst of the desert.

The author and environmentalist Aldo Leopold paddled the delta in 1922 and wrote eloquently about its abundance in his classic book, *A Sand County Almanac*: "The river was nowhere and everywhere, for he could not decide which of a hundred green lagoons offered the most pleasant and least speedy path to the Gulf." He described a river meandering through "awesome jungles," a sky turned black with birds, and visits from bobcats, racoons, and coyotes. This biological wealth stemmed from the river's natural flow regime. Annual spring floods would spread water, nutrients, and seeds throughout the floodplain, supporting lush forests and creating enticing habitat for winged, finned, and four-legged creatures.

But even in Leopold's lifetime, humans had their sights set on taming the delta. As Leopold noted sadly, "I am told the green lagoons now raise cantaloupes." He resolved never to visit the delta again, unwilling to face the devastation that humans had wrought on the landscape that so enchanted him.

Now, Jon and I set out to see what remained of the luscious green lagoons Leopold described. By that point, we had heard the river's flow was severely reduced in places, but we were still holding out hope that we would find enough water to paddle to the sea. We believed we might see a hint of what Leopold witnessed.

In early December, we crossed the border into Mexico at San Luis Rio Colorado to see what we could find. We had no idea about the toxic foam pit we were about to encounter.

The Morelos Dam is the last major dam on the main stem of the Colorado, diverting up to 1.5 million acre-feet of water into an irrigation network bound for Mexico, representing that country's allotment from a 1944 treaty. Since the treaty didn't make an allotment for the river itself, and since drought has eliminated any potential surplus, the Colorado River turns into a trickle downstream of the dam, little more than groundwater seepage. When a cab driver dropped us off at a bridge just a few miles downstream from the dam, the riverbed still had running water in it—albeit a relative trickle.

"Heck yeah!" I shouted. "We're gonna paddle this baby today."

Jon and I traded high fives and inflated our packrafts, giddy with the possibility that we might actually paddle to the sea.

We should have known better.

We lazily paddled this unexpected flow for a couple of miles before we found ourselves screeching to a stop in the frothy pit of garbage I described at the beginning of this book. The river had officially given up the ghost.

"What *is* this stuff?" Jon said. He hopped out of his raft, and I winced as I saw first one foot and then the other sink into the toxic brown muck, which reeked of fertilizer runoff and who knew what else. I'm no germaphobe, but I felt a lurch of concern. Would Jon and I get sick from touching what Jon would later describe in his book *Running Dry* as "malodorous gravy"?

"This looks like the end of the line," I said. "Guess we made it to the garbage disposal at the end of the river."

I couldn't believe that this was it. The mighty Colorado whose headwaters I had photographed in the high mountains, whose oxbows and meanders I'd marveled at from the sky, whose lettuce I had eaten and water I had drunk, simply sputtered out at this lonely place in the desert, without so much as a plaque to commemorate its demise. The indignity of the river's death disturbed me. After all the river had done for us, we let it end its journey in a soup of garbage, forgotten and unloved. It wasn't right.

My chest tightened. I felt something like nausea wash over me, and it wasn't from the rotting garbage. It was something deeper—grief mixed with bewilderment. I had to sit down on the cracked riverbank, camera in my lap, and just breathe for a few minutes.

"I thought this trip was going to be fun," I said to Jon. "But it's breaking my heart."

Although in many ways this felt like the end of our journey, Jon and I still had nearly a hundred miles to walk before we reached the sea. We deflated our rafts, packed them back up, and started walking under the scorching sun, without a coyote, beaver, or waterfowl in sight. I thought of the cottonwood groves and jaguars that used to be here, and felt despair. Where the river used to meander in green lagoons, there was now dry, cracked earth as far as the eye could see. Even the soundscape felt empty and dead. In the distance, mountains formed a pale blue oasis-like glimmer in the distance. The weight of the packraft combined with my camera gear, camping supplies, and our dromedaries of drinking water made for a crushing burden. My knees felt like they would buckle under the weight—and the thought of trudging across the Sonoran Desert for a week made my head spin.

When Jon and I set out to document the Colorado, we didn't know exactly what we'd find. But I never imagined we'd witness the total death of the river. After talking to local fishermen and farmers, we learned the truth: the river hadn't flowed to the sea since 1998.

Not a drop of it. It had dried up in my lifetime.

There is something deeply dystopian about carrying a packraft through a dry riverbed where 140-foot-long steamboats used to glide. I thought back to the Grand Ditch diversion, up in the headwaters nearly 1,500 miles behind us—the first in a long line of straws that had sucked this river dry. I thought of every ranch, lettuce farm, sprinkler, fountain, faucet, mine, golf course, and power plant that had taken its "rightful" sip from the river, leaving nothing for the river itself. All of those users were only taking what was lawfully theirs, and in many cases they were using it wisely—and yet it had still resulted in this wasteland at the end.

～

For the next week or so, Jon and I covered about fifteen miles a day. The first few days we trudged slowly under the desert sun, falling off our pace. But one day, I saw a farmer in the distance, dropped my pack, and walked over to ask if I could buy some drinking water from him. Jon and I were running low due to our heavy packs and slower-than-expected pace. He graciously agreed, but only if we joined him for a taco. Over some spicy carne asada, cilantro, and salsa on homemade tortillas at his humble adobe home, I explained our mission to him in Spanish. He laughed—and asked, "¿Por qué no estás remando?" (Why aren't you paddling?)

"El río está seco," I said. The river is dry. He laughed again, then pointed to a small lip in his field and told us to paddle there. Jon and I walked over and quickly found our new path. There was the last of the Colorado River, flowing in concrete-lined irrigation canals. We started paddling down this network of canals running alongside farmers' fields. One evening, kids were fishing in the canal as we paddled past. It was as strange for them to see us paddling as it was for us to see them fishing with throw nets in agricultural water. But for us, it was the only way to actually float since the natural river was long gone—although eventually even those concrete ditches would become too small to float.

Friends had warned us that we would be traveling through cartel country, so in addition to the sunburned, thirsty, demoralizing days looking for sludgy, shrinking canals to paddle on, we also had to contend with some anxious nights bedded down in a weed-filled wasteland in the middle of nowhere.

One night, I was jolted awake by the sound of snarling next to my head. A pack of wild dogs had surrounded our camp, barking and snapping at my sleeping bag. Jon was a tad safer as he had chosen to use a tent. I didn't have one. One of the dogs had found our food bag and was ripping it open.

"Hey!" I shouted, scrambling to my feet and looking for something to throw at them. "Get outta here!"

One of the dogs growled and snarled at me, and for a moment I thought he would attack. Then Jon started banging our metal cooking pot against a rock, and after some more barking the dogs backed off and melted into the night. Neither of us could fall back asleep. The experience only added to the general sense of doom. The land felt cursed. If the only creatures that could eke out a living here now were wild dogs, we humans had only ourselves to blame.

~

After a few more days, Jon's feet were so red and swollen he couldn't fit them into his shoes. The foul Frappuccino water had given him a serious infection, and his teeth chattered as he struggled to maneuver his raft. We called a halt and hiked out to the nearest road, where we waited to hitch a ride. After an hour, a pickup truck stopped and loaded our dusty souls into the back. They dropped us in Mexicali, where we licked our wounds in the first hotel we could find. Four weeks later, however, we returned to the delta to finish the job. After a few more days of paddling through fetid sludge and stumbling across the dried-up corpse of what used to be a thriving wetland, we arrived at the sea.

This time, we were too devastated to give each other high fives.

"I can't believe this is how it ends," Jon said.

As for me, I felt like I was staring at some apocalyptic future—the kind of thing you'd see in a movie. Except the future was the present, and there was seemingly nothing I could do.

That night, I called my parents from another hotel room.

"I feel like I've seen things I can never unsee," I said, my voice on the edge of tears. "The canals, the mining, the garbage. We've taken one of the greatest rivers in the world and just run it into the ground."

"Oh Peto," said my mom. "It sounds like you need a good night's sleep."

"I'm not just tired," I said. "I'm angry. Humans aren't stupid. We *know* what we're doing to the river. It's amazing how we ignore things just because they're out of sight. Not enough people are *seeing* this river dry up. If the Colorado River ended in a suburb of San Diego, there would have been public outcry—and I bet it would be flowing again today."

My dad's voice came through the speaker: "Peto, keep at it. You know what to do with frustration? Use it. Channel it into something meaningful. You've found a story to tell—so tell it."

Chapter 2

Sacred and Scarce

A few months after running my packraft into that fetid sludge with Jon, I found myself standing waist-deep in a completely different river, watching a partially decomposed, bloated human body float past me in the muddy current.

"Should we call the police?" I asked Madhav, my Hindu guide, trying to keep the alarm out of my voice.

"Totally normal," he said. "People bring their dead to the Ganges every day. It is a great blessing to give your body to its waters."

This wasn't what I expected when I'd pitched a story to *National Geographic* to document India's most sacred river. But then again, nothing about the Ganges was what I'd expected.

After our heartbreaking, life-changing trip down the Colorado, Jon and I published a book together called *The Colorado River: Flowing Through Conflict*, and I released a short film about the experience called *Chasing Water*. The work was getting a surprising amount of attention. Copies of our book were being passed out at Colorado River water policy meetings, and the Mexican coalition was using my photos to show US delegates just how dire things were getting south of the border. Reporters had started calling me up asking me to give a quote or two for their articles about the river, environmental groups asked if they could book me for keynote talks, and NPR's *All Things Considered* did a piece with me on their national broadcast, as if I was some kind of expert. Without quite intending to, I had started to transform from an adventure photographer to a conservation storyteller and freshwater advocate.

But the adventurous life of an itinerant photographer still called to me. I hadn't yet realized that my work on the Colorado River wasn't finished. Instead, I convinced myself I needed to understand if what we'd done to the Colorado was inevitable—if people would always suck a river dry if given the chance. It seemed to me that a lot of the problems I'd seen on my trip with Jon came from disrespecting the river, stripping it of its dignity and sacredness.

So I went looking for a river that was still considered sacred by the majority of the population relying on it, to see if the story there was different.

~

The Ganges River starts in the Garhwal Himalayas, drops over fourteen thousand feet, and flows more than fifteen hundred miles from its source at the Gangotri glacier to the Bay of Bengal. It is the same length as the Colorado, but carries fifty times more water and supports four hundred million people instead of forty million.

For nearly a billion Hindus in India and beyond, the Ganges is more than a river. It is an extension of the divine—Lord Shiva. This sacred waterway carries the prayers of believers, provides sustenance for hundreds of millions of people, supports vast industries and agriculture, and is home to endangered wildlife like

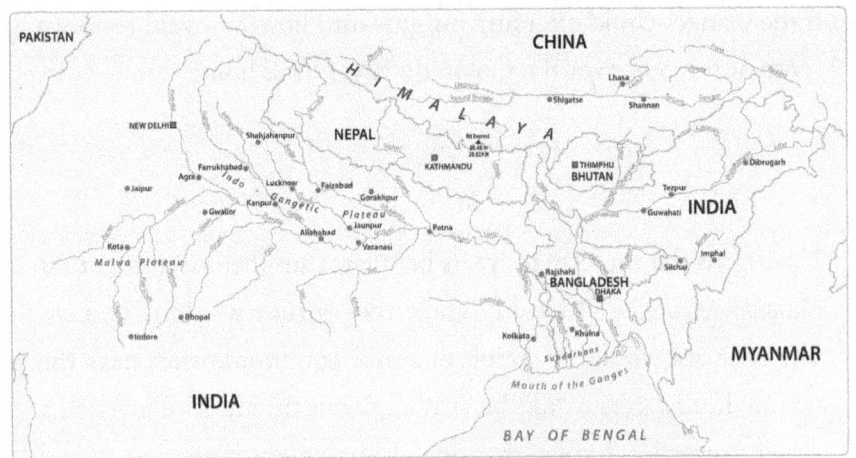

The Ganges River originates in the Garhwal Himalayas and flows southeast across India to the Bay of Bengal.

the Bengal tiger and the Ganges river dolphin, a blind freshwater dolphin called *susu* locally. To the local population it is most commonly known as Ma Ganga—Mother Ganga.

As a river lover, exploring this great place was a dream that had tantalized me for years. So in the fall of 2013, I traveled with professional climbers Jake Norton and Dave Morton to India.

The idea was simple: Climb to the top of the Ganges watershed and follow its flow through the Himalayas, across the Gangetic Plain, and through the Ganges Delta to where it kisses the ocean. The goal was to document the river and the world around it and measure the water quality en route. By traveling every mile of this sacred river on foot, by boat and aircraft, on bikes and rickshaws, and buses and trains—and even by camel, yak, and an option to ride an elephant (I opted to walk beside it)—I hoped to understand its spiritual, ecological, and cultural significance, as well as to unravel some of its paradoxes. I also wanted to find out if the Ganges could offer any insights into how we could restore a sense of reverence for the Colorado River back home.

Having visited the Ganges years before on another assignment for *National Geographic*, I already knew the journey wouldn't be easy. The logistics would be perplexing and communication near the remote headwaters would be virtually nonexistent. Moreover, as a visual storyteller, I knew that one of my biggest challenges would be determining where to point my lens in the midst of the beauty, rawness, and messy vitality that makes up India's tapestry of life.

I wanted to capture the passion and reverence that the Indian people exhibited for their beloved waterway as they went there to pray, to bathe, and to admire its power. Unlike many rivers worldwide, the public in India embrace their river with open arms. People pray on its banks daily, along the entire length of the watershed. In the holy cities of Rishikesh, Haridwar, and Varanasi, formal prayer services called the Ganga Aarti occur every day, complete with music, fire, and speeches. Some call it the "Hindu happy hour."

This collective spiritual hug given by the hundreds of millions using the river comes with costs. Pollution and a lack of environmental awareness are visible across much of the watershed. And in many areas, these challenges are compounded by a mindset common to those who revere the river's sacred flow. To them, the river is God—thus it is all-powerful and immune to the threats of overuse, contamination, and environmental degradation. In short, people believe the curative powers of the Ganges will heal not only them, but the river itself.

This is the paradox of this mighty river, which sparks a key question: If the physical river dies, what happens to its spiritual power?

～

Working on assignment as a National Geographic Explorer grantee, I met up with Jake and Dave in Rishikesh and then traveled for two days by vehicle via washed-out roads to Gangotri. We began our trek on the heels of a record monsoon that triggered a glacial outburst flood, which taught us our first river lesson—the Ganges gives and the Ganges takes away. Over six thousand people died in the flooding and thousands more were reported missing. Miles of roads were washed out and complete hillsides scoured naked. Entire villages were swept into oblivion. The communities we traveled through mourned with stoic resilience. As we plodded north, I began to wonder if our plan was prudent. The river gods—Hindu and otherwise—appeared to be far from happy.

Just before sunset, snow started to fall in wet, heavy flakes. Jake looked up and said, as much to the sky as to us, "This feels like one of those monsoon storms that stick around." But there was nothing to do except button up. We were high in the Garhwal region, at roughly 17,500 feet atop the giant Gangotri glacier, surrounded by 23,000-foot peaks, many unclimbed. It had taken us nearly ten days to get there—six of them walking through treacherous glacial moraine. We were miles from any whisper of civilization. And, due to our proximity to India's northwestern border with Pakistan, satellite phones were prohibited. We were acutely aware that any rescue by helicopter was out of the question.

We had come to this remote spot with the intention of clawing our way up the unclimbed Chaukhamba IV, a 22,487-foot glacier-clad granite monster. Avalanche conditions were ripe, however, so we targeted a 22,200-foot peak just to the west and positioned ourselves to move upward the next day. As darkness closed in, the wet, heavy flakes of snow changed to hail, and we lay in our sleeping bags cracking jokes about our situation, intently focused on the sound of the storm.

All through the night, we continually shook accumulating snow from our tents and took turns shoveling every two hours to keep the ventilation from sealing closed. The steady creaks and moans of the glacier that had kept me awake on previous nights had subsided, and the steady roar of water pouring down the glacier had gone mute. All we heard was the icy hail tap-dancing on our tent.

Sometime around midnight, a new sound jolted us awake. A low rumble, like distant thunder. *An avalanche.* At first, we heard it from afar—high up on Chaukhamba. But the rumbling steadily grew louder. We looked at each other. "How far are we from the mountain?" I asked, starting to eye my boots. Jake assured me we were fine. Ten minutes later, we heard another roar, even louder, causing Jake to eye his own boots.

For the next five hours, the avalanches continued, their sounds varying between that of distant thunderstorms and the crack of artillery fire. Throughout the night, we counted thirty-six. I remembered some advice my local guide Madhav had once given me: "Don't worry so much," he'd said. "Remember, worry is praying for what you don't want." Good advice, but here in the remoteness of the Himalayas, it was hard not to worry some. At 5:30 in the morning, we came to the conclusion that our climbing mission was over. Over the next six hours, we battled our way through thigh-deep, concrete-like snow, finally arriving at our base camp the following night so tired we could barely eat. The tents we had left were flattened and destroyed by the heavy snow.

Feeling somewhat defeated by our abandoned climb, we pushed downstream past Gaumukh, "the cow's mouth," where the Ganges pours out from beneath the collapsing foot of the Gangotri glacier. This transition from ice to river is spiritually powerful, and many Hindus come here as pilgrims. Unfortunately, this key transition point is also moving upstream at a rate of roughly sixty feet a year—climate change at work.

After weeks on foot, we returned to wheeled travel in four-wheel-drive vehicles, moving downstream through the scoured canyons of a gravity-fueled river. The roads that were washed out when we came in were now repaired, barely. "It feels like we're driving on a sandcastle," said Dave.

When we entered the lower foothills, the Tehri Dam and reservoir, one of the largest and most controversial hydroelectric projects in the world, stretched before us. To quench a growing thirst for electricity, the Tehri project had submerged forty villages and physically stopped Lord Shiva's flow. The Tehri dam reservoir only flooded 20 square miles of land, compared with 254 square miles that were flooded to create Lake Powell. Still, to the nearly one hundred thousand people forced out of their homes, it was devastating. I wondered what had happened to those people—how they had coped with the loss of not only their physical houses but their spiritual ties to a place that was gone forever. Thinking of that displacement reminded me of the hundreds of Native cultural sites drowned beneath Lake Powell. I wondered if any of them remained in the cold water below.

―

With the Ganges's sacred headwaters behind us, we traveled downstream to Varanasi to visit the famous ghats (stone steps) where thousands of human bodies are cremated and their ashes strewn into the river each year. In India, people face death directly, the same way they face their beloved river, as polluted as it may be. In the US, we tend to put both these things out of our minds and wait to confront them only when they become too pressing to ignore.

Few funeral practices are as transparent and raw as the Hindu ritual that plays out on the banks of the Ganges. Hindus believe that if the ashes of the deceased are laid in the Ganges at Varanasi, their souls will be transported to heaven and escape the cycle of rebirth. In a culture that believes in reincarnation, this concept, called moksha, is profound. The holier the place, the better the chances are that an individual can achieve moksha and avoid returning in the next life as a cow or a cricket.

Since many believe Varanasi has been inhabited for five thousand years (which would make it one of the world's oldest cities), it is considered to be the most sacred city on the banks of the Ganges. People come from all over to pray, collect sacred water, bathe, and, yes, attend to their dead. Some even come to die.

Thanks to Madhav, our team was given permission to document these sacred rituals.

Within minutes of stepping onto Varanasi's famous cremation ghat, sweat was streaming down my face. My teammates, who were filming next to me, struggled to breathe in the blasting heat. I could barely see through my camera lens. I asked our guide Raj, who had worked his entire life on the burning ghat, if he ever got used to the heat.

"What heat?" he joked. "Yes, we do. We help those make the passage at the end. It is beautiful, no?"

Like most things in India, however, a parallel story was unfolding alongside this ritual of death. The demand for wood, particularly hardwood, is negatively impacting Himalayan forests. Burning just one large body can require more than one thousand pounds of logs. In fact, fifty to sixty million trees are consumed annually in India alone. Electric or gas-fired crematoria have been built, but both depend on unreliable energy sources and so most families still prefer traditional methods.

As the sun continued to rise, I noticed three boats carrying towering loads of timber coming downstream. Raj pointed out one electrical crematorium nearby. It was closed.

Not everyone can afford the cost of funeral pyres. Even the cheapest wood is beyond reach for many of the poor. As a result, many bodies are discarded into the Ganges only partially cremated or not at all. It is estimated that one hundred thousand bodies in various stages of cremation are consigned to the Ganges each year.

By 9:00 that morning, with the Indian sun blazing above the Ganges, three fires were burning. My hair was covered in ash and I was once again soaked in sweat. As I walked through the area where workers were splitting wood, an old woman suddenly emerged from the shadows and held out her hand, the international request for money. Raj casually observed: "She lives here. Her family left her. She has come to die and needs money for cremation. Want to donate some rupees for her wood?"

≈

To get a better grasp of the river's health, we had been testing the water quality along our entire journey. The results in many locations were as expected, showing spikes in heavy metals and nitrates. And in certain troubled areas, oxygen levels plummeted. On the Yamuna River, the largest tributary of the Ganges, which carries the runoff of New Delhi's economic boom, we tested a section flowing past the Taj Mahal in Agra. We waded out into the garbage and sewage, to confirm, with data, what our senses were already screaming: The Yamuna River in Agra is far from healthy and full of waste of every putrid kind. Not surprisingly, the river registered zero dissolved oxygen. It was a dead river.

And yet, when we rejoined the Yamuna at Allahabad some three hundred miles downstream and roughly halfway down the Ganges, our samples showed dissolved oxygen levels similar to those found in healthy rivers, although heavy metal levels remained high. Somehow, someway, the Ganges was restoring itself. Perhaps, as many people believe, there are some curative powers or obscure minerals that support the river's health.

According to Julian Crandall Hollick at NPR, the British East India Company only used Ganges water on their three-month-long journeys home to England because it stayed "sweet and fresh."

Scientists point to the unusually high levels of bacteriophages—viruses known to eat bacteria and keep disease at bay—found in the river's water as a potential explanation. But no one can definitively say where and why the antibacterial properties originate ("Mystery Factor Gives Ganges a Clean Reputation," NPR, December 16, 2007). As early as 1896, British scientists documented thriving cholera bacteria dying when put into Ganges water. And experts have yet to fully explain the river's ability to sustain and revive its high oxygen levels. Whatever the reason why, the river has endured for centuries.

Throughout our journey, when I asked how the river was able to restore its oxygen levels, many people fell back on a spiritual answer. Ma Ganga, India's national river, is sacred—the creation of Lord Shiva himself, the Hindu god of destruction. Of course the river can kill bacteria!

But even a god might blanch at the ecological challenges facing this river. Five of the twenty most polluted cities in the world sit in the basin of the Ganges. The river suffers from vast dead zones spanning hundreds of miles that show seventy times the recommended maximum level of heavy metals, in part due to the leather-tanning industry. I couldn't help but think that the local attitude of the river's ability to heal itself was wishful spiritual thinking; I knew the truth—that the overall health of the river, in many ways, couldn't be worse.

Back in the United States, of course, we have our own version of wishful thinking: the belief that we can engineer our way around the basic laws of physics, and keep on allocating more water than the Colorado actually carries. We tell ourselves our water problems can be solved by more dams, that new housing developments in the desert will find water one way or another, and that the economic costs of cutting back on water usage are just too high to justify making change. We tell ourselves that next year there will be more snowpack or heavier rain. Instead of touting the river's ability to heal itself, we put too much faith in our own ability to squeeze water from desert rocks, telling ourselves we can outsmart the ecological truths that are staring us in the face.

Yet despite my awareness of these different versions of denial, I sometimes found myself feeling a little envious of the intimate relationship Indians had with their river.

Yes, my science-based upbringing made it hard to accept the spiritual response to questions about the river's health—but I was frequently moved by the Indian people's open-armed reverence for the river and its healing powers. In India, although people interact with the Ganges daily—playing, working, praying, and grieving on its shores—civic concern for abusing the river is almost entirely nonexistent. Most believe Ma Ganga will repair itself. One woman told me, "Babies defecate in their mothers' laps all the time and the mother cleans it. The Ganges is our mother. It is no different."

This paradoxical thinking perplexed me along every river mile we traveled. Those who revere the great Ganges the most pollute it equally. And yet, many of those same believers complain that the Ganges is dirty—too polluted even to swim in anymore.

Despite all I had seen floating in the Ganges, I swam or waded in it almost everywhere we went. Crazy, perhaps, but I wanted to experience the river firsthand, as the locals did. Did I get sick? Yes, but not from swimming. (I got food poisoning after eating fish at a fancy restaurant.) Did I feel that my sins were washed away? I'm not sure, but I did feel invigorated after every dip.

Moving downriver from Varanasi, we arrived in Kanpur, the center of the leather-tanning industry. As we walked inside one of the tanneries, I could taste metal in my gums. I recognized ammonia, then something else I couldn't identify. Before the thought had a chance to linger, all of my senses were overwhelmed. My nostrils burned, my eyes watered, my throat became raw. I looked back at our crew and saw that everyone was waging a similar battle—blinking their eyes, covering their mouths, and fighting the urge to turn around and leave. The cool, misty air of the Himalayan foothills, some three hundred miles upstream, was a distant dream.

Despite my now-burning sinuses, watering eyes, and increasing nausea, I was right where I wanted to be—deep inside one of the most controversial industries on the banks of the Ganges. It had taken us four weeks to get here and two days of negotiations to gain access.

Leather textiles are part of Kanpur's DNA, but the industry is a sensitive political issue. During British rule, Kanpur developed on the banks of the Ganges because textile companies could transport their goods to market easily from there. In 2009, India was producing 8 percent of the world's leather supply, and leather remains an economic engine for the region. Much of it is used to manufacture shoes. When I asked one worker if my lightweight hiking boots were made of Kanpur leather, he smiled and said "Yes, very likely."

Despite their economic success, however, tanneries have been severely criticized for polluting water supplies—specifically the Ganges—with heavy metals like chromium, a hardening agent in

Workers process hides at a tannery in Kanpur.

leather production. Improperly handled, chromium can be a nasty business. It is linked to lung cancer, liver failure, kidney damage, and premature dementia. I noticed the shirtless workers in front of me and worried for their health.

I remembered all the mining ponds I had seen from the air when my dad and I were flying around Colorado in his Cessna. From the cockpit, those ponds had looked almost beautiful—like abstract art. I'd made dozens of photographs. But up close in Kanpur, faced with the reality of what those heavy metals do to human bodies and ecosystems, I was shocked to think about what those mines might be discharging back into the Colorado River. While both the tanneries and the molybdenum mines were technically governed by environmental regulations, it was clear that what happened on paper was often a much different story than what took place in real life.

There are approximately four hundred tanneries operating in Kanpur today—even after some seventy others were shuttered due to pollution concerns. Those remaining are required to recycle all their water. Both the facilities we visited, one large and one small, had recycling systems, but both required electricity to run their pumps. And electricity production is notoriously unreliable in northern India, with power outages occurring six to eight times a day. When the power goes down, milky silver-gray water spills into overflow ditches in the streets, most likely headed for the river.

The water samples we took from the river at Kanpur were later tested for twenty-one heavy metals at a registered drinking-water test facility in Denver, Colorado. Not surprisingly, our samples showed a steep spike in chromium—some of the highest heavy-metal levels we recorded. This was not an anomaly. In 2013, one study reported that these tanneries were pumping thirty crore liters (roughly seventy-nine million gallons) of contaminated water into the Ganges every day, while the city's treatment facility could handle only seventeen crore liters (about forty-five million gallons) per day.

Later, my teammate Jake and I photographed children playing among chromium-laden leather scraps on the banks of the river. It was a joyous scene, full of laughter and energy. As the sun set, I looked out at the lazy, chai-colored flow of the Ganges. Surprisingly, no one arrived for evening prayer, as we had consistently seen upstream throughout the terraced farmlands of the Himalayan foothills. I assumed that was because we were in a predominantly Muslim section of the city where the Ganges wasn't considered to be spiritually significant. In fact, I witnessed few Hindus visiting the river anywhere in Kanpur—just one family doing laundry and some teenagers breakdancing. After teaching me a few Indian moves, the breakers told me they were Hindu and that they sometimes prayed to Ganga, but they never swam or bathed there. "It's too dirty," they complained.

～

After chasing the sacred Ganges 1,550 miles, from nearly 18,000 feet and a frigid −20 degrees down to sea level and 110-degree heat, we reached the end of our journey at Sagar Island. A cyclone had just subsided and the sun struggled to emerge. I weighed thirty pounds less than when we had started.

The air was humid and sweltering, and nothing seemed more fitting than going bodysurfing. Jake, Dave, and I sprinted out to greet the small, glassy swell rolling onto the beach. The brackish water was bathtub warm, but felt delightfully cooler than the air. A pack of children quickly joined us, and laughter echoed across the bay.

As we played in the waves, I recalled the desolate spot in Mexico where the Colorado River used to drain into the sea. The contrast was profound. Despite all the pollution, dams, diversions, and thirsty industries, the Ganges completed its journey without drying up, although it does come very close in certain sections. I wondered if there was something in the Hindu reverence for the Ganges—something missing from our Western relationship with water—that had protected it from the ultimate hubris: stopping a major river from reaching the ocean entirely. Of course, there were also environmental factors that gave the Ganges a heavier flow.

Still, despite all the devotion we had witnessed, I had to wonder if people would ever realize a simple truth: Sacred and unique as it may be, this river will need more than prayer to survive. After washing the sins of so many for so long, India will eventually have to clean the sins of industry, agriculture, and devoted love thrown daily into the lap of their national mother, Ma Ganga.

～

The Ganges is anything but out of sight, out of mind—whereas for many Americans who depend on it, the Colorado River is something they may never visit at all, much less consider sacred.

Flying home, I couldn't shake the parallels between these two rivers: one sacred in name but defiled in practice, the other one stripped of its sacredness while providing critical services to millions. We were asking so much from both, while failing to consider what the rivers themselves might need to thrive.

It wasn't lost on me, either, that both of the river trips I'd just taken had featured ashes: Jon's mother's at the Colorado headwaters, and countless others at the burning ghats in Varanasi. Life was short; I would only have so many expeditions to go on and stories to tell before my own body was turned to ash. I had a feeling that more and more of those stories would have to do with rivers, and especially those closer to home.

I had no idea just how accurate that hunch would prove to be.

Chapter 3

Delta Dawn

I'd sworn I'd never go back to the Colorado River delta. The place had nearly broken me. And yet in March 2014 I found myself in the exact same spot where Jon and I had watched the river sputter out—only now it was flowing with fresh water, and I was getting ready to float down what had once been a dry wash.

Soon after I got back from India, I'd started getting emails and phone calls from friends.

Rowan Jacobson, a writer for *Outside* magazine, was one of them.

"Pete, have you heard about the pulse flow they're planning for the Colorado River delta?" he said.

"I've heard and read a little, but can you update me on the latest?" I asked.

"They're going to give some of the water back to the river," he explained. "The point is to mimic a spring flood, like the kind that would have soaked the delta every year."

I tried to imagine steely-eyed water managers in Nevada and Arizona willingly giving up some water so that the river itself could get a sip. I have to admit—I was skeptical.

"Are you kidding me?" I said. "How much water are we talking?"

"About 105,000 acre-feet over eight weeks."

I scoffed. "That *sounds* like a lot, but in the big picture it's almost nothing. What is that, like 2 percent of what the delta would have gotten before we put in all the dams?"

I could hear him wincing through the phone. "Actually, 1 percent. But hear me out. Even 1 percent might be enough to germinate a few seeds, bring back a few fish, attract a few birds."

My heart started pounding. I realized there was one big question that mattered to me more than all the others. "Is it going to reach the sea?"

There was a long pause. "I can't make any promises," said Rowan. "But who knows—it just might."

Lying in bed that night, I felt myself at a crossroads. After India, I'd wanted to keep doing international assignments, focusing my lenses on the major rivers of the world. But the Colorado was calling—again. My trip with Jon had ended so traumatically. Now, here was a chance to go back to the site of that heartbreak and see something beautiful happen—or at least *try* to happen. Maybe if I paddled the Colorado all the way to the sea, the part of me that had broken in that dry and abandoned delta could be healed.

When I told my dad I was planning another trip to the delta, he laughed.

"You're turning into quite the river advocate," he said. "How much are they paying you for this trip?"

"Standard assignment day rates, which isn't a lot, but enough to cover travel expenses and save a few bucks," I admitted. "Basic burritos—maybe with guacamole—will be as fancy as I get."

"Moving up in the world," he chuckled.

When I first told my parents I wanted to be an adventure photographer—just months after graduating from Dartmouth College with a degree in English and environmental studies—my dad tried to convince me to choose a more practical career. "You're not going to make a living," he said, remembering his own disheartening attempts to sell ski movies. I knew that by trying to talk me out of photography he was just being practical and doing what dads do, the same way his own father had tried to talk him out of moving to that "nowhere town" in Colorado to build a cabin and be a ski bum.

I remember telling him early on that I had to try it and he needed to trust me. "Remember," I said, "You didn't exactly follow the career in finance your father suggested for you, either."

In my first year of trying to make it as a photographer, I only made about fourteen thousand dollars, when my cost of living was thirteen thousand dollars (I didn't have health insurance). Still, I was damn proud. Slowly, I built up to bigger and bigger assignments, and my dad came to accept that I wouldn't be switching to a more practical career anytime soon.

"You know, Dad," I said, "so much of my work lately has been looking at ecosystems we've abused. This is a chance to see something different—people coming together to bring an ecosystem back to life."

My dad was silent for a moment.

"You can't fool me, Peto," he said. "We all know you're hoping to paddle that river to the sea—and I applaud you for trying."

—

In the months before I traveled back to Mexico for the pulse flow, I read all I could about the river's natural flooding cycle. Before all the dams and reservoirs, the Colorado would have flooded every spring, charged up with runoff from melting snow in the mountains. This yearly deluge replenished the groundwater, flushed salt from the soil, and carried fertile muck up to the floodplains. The rushing water carried a wealth of nutrients for fish to gorge on, while the silt left behind created the perfect nurseries for them to lay their eggs. The water jolted dormant seeds awake and made trees and bushes explode with vibrant green growth for deer and other animals to munch on.

A pulse flow in the Colorado River delta would mean cottonwood fluff dancing on the breeze and tender green shoots in an ocean of cracked earth. It would mean birds and fish drawn by abundant food and habitat. It would mean a celebration for all the people in Mexico who still remembered a time when a living river flowed through their backyards—and for the younger generations for whom this river was little more than the stuff of legend. Maybe it would even mean the first step in restoring a long-neglected ecosystem—if not to its former glory, then at least to something better than the hellscape to which we had reduced it.

I was falling head over heels for this pulse flow, and I hadn't even seen it yet. When I imagined the delta rippling with water,

Cracked earth spreads across the dry
Colorado River delta as far as the eye can see.

birds flying overhead and green leaves rustling in the breeze, I felt some youthful, electric excitement I hadn't felt in years.

Nevertheless, I tempered my starry-eyed enthusiasm. I reminded myself that nobody was talking about restoring the delta—just giving it a tiny sip of water. After eight weeks, the tap would be turned off again, and the river would dry back up. In fact, some people were already writing it off as a publicity stunt before it even happened. I tuned out those voices. Couldn't they see how monumental this was? The United States and Mexico had come to the first binational agreement to give a little water back to the river—and in an era when every drop was bitterly contested, that was practically impossible.

The truth is, I was becoming somewhat fixated. The Colorado River and its fate were consuming more and more of my focus. What had begun as a way to spend quality time flying with my dad was now something more personal—a responsibility I couldn't shirk. The Colorado had become the lens through which I viewed other rivers; indeed, it was becoming the lens through which I viewed life, providing endless metaphors for time, resilience, memory, and loss.

On the day the pulse flow began, farmworkers labored in nearby fields, harvesting produce and moving irrigation pipes, their schedules dictated by moisture and sun. It was a typical Sunday, but just a few minutes after 8:00 a.m. something very atypical happened. A set of giant control wheels on the Morelos Dam, unmoved for decades, started screeching, cranking open the red steel gates of the last major blockade on the Colorado River. As the rusty doors lifted, a titanic surge of greenish-brown water raced south, swirling and eddying down a riverbed that had sat parched and empty since the late 1990s.

There was something surreal about watching those gates open up. To restore life to the delta, all we had to do was open a door—and yet this simple act represented the culmination of years of painstaking diplomatic negotiations, scientific research, and advocacy work by dozens of organizations on both sides of the border. I found myself asking a question that would gain urgency throughout my years documenting the Colorado River: Why is it so hard to do the right thing? We know that rivers need water—so why is it so hard for us to let them run?

Of course, the answer extends far back into history. In 1944, the United States and Mexico signed a water treaty governing how water from the Colorado and Rio Grande rivers would be managed. For years, both countries had been developing more and more farms in dry, dusty places, and these farms needed irrigation water to survive. As the United States ramped up dam-building projects throughout the 1920s and '30s, including the massive Hoover Dam, less and less water from the Colorado River was making its way to Mexico—and the Mexicans were understandably peeved. While American farms were booming thanks to the new dams and reservoirs, farms in Mexico were turning into dust bowls. Something had to give.

In the early 1940s, World War II was reshaping global politics and making strong alliances more important than ever. President Roosevelt recognized that Mexico was an important ally to the US; nothing good could come of angering this giant neighbor by hoarding all the river water and only letting a small trickle over the border. Mexico had also become an important source of farm labor to the US thanks to the Bracero Program, begun in 1942, which allowed Mexican laborers into the country on a temporary basis to work on farms and railroads.

Still, despite all the talk of friendship and unity, the United States had the upper hand in negotiations, and this is reflected in the treaty. At the end of the day, the US agreed to give Mexico 1.5 million acre-feet of Colorado River water per year—which may sound like a lot but is actually far less than states like California were using. Meanwhile, Mexico agreed to deliver 350,000 acre-feet of water per year from six tributaries into the Rio Grande.

The treaty basically guaranteed that the US could continue building sprawling farms and cities in the arid Southwest, regardless of whether it made ecological sense to do so. As the downstream water user, and with infrastructure like the Hoover Dam already a done deal, the best Mexico could do was secure a minimum water guarantee.

Over the ensuing decades, this treaty has been put to the test over and over again. In Roosevelt's time, nobody was predicting the megadroughts we see today. Nobody realized that factors like decreased snowpack and lower river flows would make it much harder or even impossible for either country to fulfill its treaty obligations. At different moments, farmers on both sides of the border have felt outraged to see "their" water being given away to the other country in times of dire need. Farmers in Mexico have complained that the Colorado River water they receive from the US is contaminated with high levels of salt, which stunts their crops and leaves crusty white patches on the soil; farmers in Texas have sued for stronger enforcement when Mexico falls behind on its Rio Grande deliveries.

But the biggest problem with the US–Mexico water treaty is that it was only designed with humans in mind, with zero consideration given to the river itself—or to the plants and animals that depend on it. It's as if the people who wrote the treaty simply forgot that water had any other purpose than irrigating fields or watering lawns. This catastrophic oversight meant that millions of living things that depend on the river—from panthers to trees to tiny crustaceans—were essentially sentenced to death.

In 2012, after years of tedious meetings and sometimes-fraught discussions, officials from both sides of the border agreed on an addendum to the treaty, known as Minute 319. Among other things, this addendum called for the experimental release of what it calls "water for the environment"—a foreign concept to the people who drafted the original treaty, but a popular one among the Nature Conservancy, the Environmental Defense Fund, the

Sonoran Institute, and many more organizations who spent years advocating for the addendum.

After decades of allocating precisely zero water for the river itself, we would experiment with giving the river a tiny amount and seeing how much good it could do. This historic ripple in water policy represented a shift in thinking: rivers weren't just glorified faucets for humans to turn on and off as we saw fit, but ecosystems with their own needs, and their own right to exist.

There was a good reason scientists had allocated eight weeks for the pulse flow. Like an elderly grandparent, the newly released river would move slowly, retracing its old path step by watery step. It would take it a long time to cover roughly one hundred miles to the sea—but the small crew of river rats that rallied to join Rowan and me would be there to cheer it on.

～

Two years after the addendum passed, we finally got to see the results. In anticipation of the river's arrival, local residents gathered beneath a bridge in San Luis Rio Colorado. Ranchero music blasted from portable speakers and a festive atmosphere pervaded the crowd as they waited for the watery guest of honor to appear. With every foot the river advanced, the giddiness in the crowd increased. Families set up picnics on the riverbank, with kids splashing in the shallow water and cowboys dancing their horses through the stream; within hours of the river's arrival, fishermen were reeling in carp.

I couldn't believe this was the same place where a sense of despair and outrage had overtaken me as I deflated my raft and packed it onto my back. Looking around, I realized that this festive, colorful scene is what the rather sad, depressed town of San Luis *used* to be like before we'd stolen its river.

It was bewildering to think that these folks had been deprived of a river that brought them such joy—a river that had flowed through their community for untold generations, until diversion by diversion, dam by dam, we had dried it up. It was clear to me that people in Mexico needed this water—not just for drinking, washing, or growing crops, but for pleasure, beauty, and solace. In reducing the Colorado to a crop-watering, turbine-spinning machine, we had erased a central aspect of our own humanity. We couldn't turn our rivers into enormous plumbing systems without mechanizing ourselves, or dry up their riverbeds without parching our own souls.

Mexican cowboys dance their horses in the newly arrived river.

Watching Mexican families celebrate this slow-moving trickle of water, I was struck by my own privilege. Growing up in the high country of Colorado, near the river's headwaters, I had never questioned if there would be enough water to swim, fish, or paddle. Although there were a handful of diversions upstream of my family's ranch, we were nevertheless among the first in line to receive our allocation of water. I had never imagined what it would be like to be *last* in line—to receive a ditch full of salty, exhausted sludge, if you got anything at all. As I watched Mexican kids laughing and splashing in the long-awaited flow, I wished for their sake that the pulse flow would become a regular event.

Yet some of the scientists who rounded out our little flotilla worried that this flow would prove to be more of a symbol than a true fix. Fred Phillips, a habitat-restoration expert who specialized in wetlands, told me that this section of river was "the most forgotten in the world." For the past year, he and others had been planting native seeds and saplings in the delta, hoping that the pulse flow would cause them to grow, creating habitat for the delta's three hundred thousand migrating birds. Still, he worried that media attention would wane once the pulse flow was over—leaving many people's hopes to dry up with the delta.

"They should use the minimum amount of water for the photo op," he told me, casting a wry glance at my camera, "and the maximum amount for habitat restoration."

Fred had a point. As a photographer, I was part of the media machine that would frame this story for the outside world. Was I just here to capture dramatic before-and-after shots? Or was I bearing witness to something more profound—a glimpse of what restoration might look like if we had the will to pursue it?

Another skeptic was Sam Walton, a river guide, hydrologist, and member of the family behind Walmart. At the time, the

Walton Family Foundation was donating $25 million a year to nonprofits focused on the Colorado River, and Sam was one of the family members involved in allocating those funds. He worried that the dry riverbed would soak up the pulse flow like a sponge, before the water had a chance to make it to the restoration sites people like Fred had been carefully tending for so long. In his mind, the water should have been funneled directly to those sites in canals, instead of being allowed to meander along the riverbed, and possibly dry up along the way. He hoped that over the course of our paddleboarding adventure, he would be proven wrong.

~

As we made our way down the temporary river, those invasive tamarisk bushes I'd pushed through on foot with Jon were now deep underwater, their feathery tips brushing the bottoms of our paddleboards. We began to see and hear creatures like beavers, coyotes, and white-faced ibis, which would have been unthinkable during my hellish slog over the delta several years earlier. I couldn't believe how normal it all felt—how the land's ecological memory ran so deep that these things could simply snap back. Seeds that had lain dormant were sprouting; tiny crustaceans whose eggs had been lying in wait for years on end had finally hatched, and were now busily chomping on algae. With each plant or animal I saw, I felt a new lightness in my heart. It truly felt like witnessing a miracle.

"It's incredible how fast this is all coming back," I enthused to Fred as we watched a great blue heron stalk through the shallows. "I didn't realize it could all just spring back to life after so much abuse."

"Ecological memory's a wonderful thing," he said. "Sometimes all you need to do is remove impediments and let the systems heal themselves." He paused. "Of course, you've still got climate change, and that's one impediment we can't easily remove. Even if we left the Morelos Dam open year-round, it wouldn't change the fact that the air's getting hotter, the snowpack's getting thinner, and we've had all these invasive plants and animals move in."

As I watched nature's memory assert itself, I felt my own memory being restored as well. Paddling through green channels where I'd once trudged through dust, I remembered the joy of being carried by something bigger than myself. I remembered how, in drought years when the skiing was bad, Dad would drag my brother and sister and me up to alpine lakes to go skating. I'll never forget the thick silence of those places, broken only by the soft hushing of our blades against the ice. These, too, were memories of the watershed: in the spring, those melting lakes would feed this very river. Gliding across that frozen water, I had the sense that we were at the very top of the world—and gliding through the delta, I felt that that precious mountain water was being reunited with a long-lost friend.

~

After thirty-two miles, we found that we had run out of river. The water was still advancing, but slowly—and to our surprise, there was a giant earthen dam blocking the way. It had apparently been built by farmers so they could more easily drive their trucks across the riverbed—which, to be fair, was usually bone-dry. After I notified the pulse flow experts about the dam, we spent the night hand-digging a channel through it to let the Rio Colorado run free. We toasted the river and took turns making "butt dams" to block our little channel.

The next morning, the advancing river had eroded away much of the dam and was fighting its way through, as if determined to reach the sea.

Rowan and the others had to get back to their lives. They couldn't wait for the river to creep forward one mile at a time, especially when there were still sixty miles to go.

But I couldn't just walk away, knowing this might be my only chance to paddle the Colorado River all the way to the sea. I knew that some opportunities only come around once in a lifetime, and this was clearly one of them. As long as I lived, I might never see a wet, living, paddle-able Colorado River delta ever again.

And so I told Rowan that Sam and I had decided to keep pushing on.

For me, it had turned into a mission. Seeing the Ganges run into the ocean at Sagar Island had done something to me. Standing in that warm, brackish water where the sacred river finally kissed the bay, I'd felt a sense of completion. Despite all the pollution, all the problems, the Ganges still got to finish its journey. I'd witnessed the same on the Nile and many other rivers.

The Colorado deserved the same dignity. I *needed* to see the Colorado fulfill its destiny, even if it was just for a few moments, and even if it was just a trickle of its former self. I needed to know that something that had been so thoroughly broken by human demands could be made whole again, even if it was just for a day. And maybe there was a little bit of my own ego woven into the journey, too—I wanted to be able to say that I'd achieved my goal of paddling the Colorado to the sea—even if Sam and I were the last people in the world to do so.

～

With so little water in the riverbed, making progress meant complete warfare. Sam and I fought through jungles of cattail and mesquite, one twenty-mile push at a time. We were joined by local bird expert Juan Butron, who grew up in the delta and had seen steamships pass his house when he was young. Like us, he wanted to see what kind of rio restoration was possible. He had never paddleboarded but figured it out quickly and loved it. He did the entire journey wearing his favorite Wrangler jeans—and singing when the going got tough.

Some days, the temperature topped 107 degrees; at night, the mosquitoes were merciless. Water meant birds, crustaceans, and fish, but it also meant snakes. More than once, my body tensed as I saw a venomous coral snake glide just below my flimsy paddleboard. I was glad to see life in the river, but I hadn't counted on the extra danger it would present.

"This is an improvement, I swear," I told Sam. "When Jon and I did this, we would have *killed* for this much water to paddle in."

He looked dubious. "Remind me why we're doing this again?"

I mock cried, and we all laughed. . . . But I knew that real tears weren't too far in our future if we had to keep going like this for many more days.

Finally, in early May, Sam, Juan, and I hit the high-tide line of the Gulf of California at low tide. Sunbaked, bruised, and mosquito-bitten, we declared victory. We would be the last people to ever paddle the Colorado River to the sea. On many levels, it was a preposterous journey—foolish, even wrongheaded. "The most absurd paddleboard mission ever," as I would tell my friends.

But it was beautiful and symbolic—that with a relative trickle, we can restore a river, if we try.

By the time Sam and I left the delta, the pulse flow was coming to an end. The dancing horses and happy kids were no longer at the river's shore near San Luis. The fiesta was over. Once again, the river was back to sand. Just as the pulse reached the sea, its tail was already drying.

Like most environmental victories these days, our moment of triumph was bittersweet. We had witnessed something remarkable—the brief restoration of an ecosystem that many had written off as permanently lost. But we had also seen how tenuous that restoration was, depending on sensitive diplomatic agreements, scrupulous water accounting, and an all-too-rare decision to allocate at least some water to nature itself. Despite the pulse flow's success, everyone agreed that it was unlikely to happen again. Getting all the stakeholders to agree was just too hard, and took too long.

Back in the United States, I found myself struggling to convey the significance of what I'd witnessed. Some people were dismissing the pulse flow as a waste of precious water in an increasingly arid West. Why should we care about some bird habitat in Mexico when farmers in California were fallowing fields and cities were implementing water restrictions?

But reducing the delta to a water balance sheet misses the deeper meaning of what happened there. The pulse flow was about more than hydrology; it was about ecology, community, and the recognition that some values can't be fully captured in acre-feet calculations.

What some people forget is that rivers are better when they're wet. It's that simple. And there are a few people in Mexico who wouldn't call it a waste.

For those who saw the river dry and wet, the dam closed and open, they would say the pulse flow was a success. Having found the Colorado River bucking right where we left it, I know from experience it was an improvement.

The pulse flow didn't solve the Colorado River's problems. It didn't reverse decades of overallocation. But it reminded me that we have choices about how we use our water, and that sometimes giving a little back to the river itself pays unexpected dividends.

All I knew was that I would never forget the sight of those Mexican families celebrating the fleeting return of their beloved friend. Watching them swim, dance their horses, picnic, stroll, or just sit in lawn chairs on the bank and gaze at the rio as ranchero music lilted across the water, it occurred to me that just as the river can't speak for itself, our decisions about water disproportionately affect people whose voices have been marginalized. The people picnicking under the bridge at San Luis Rio Colorado weren't wealthy CEOs with political connections. They were workers, families, and community members who'd had their river stolen from them one drop at a time. In that sense, restoring the Colorado wasn't just about creating habitat for fish and animals, but about dispensing a drop of justice for the humans whose lives had been burned along the way.

I was starting to realize that the people most intimately connected to water are often the last to be consulted and the first to suffer when it disappears. I'd witnessed a community springing back to life along with the cottonwood seeds on the riverbank. Now, I wondered just how many other communities we'd trampled on when we set out to tame the Colorado. Little did I know, I was about to learn much more about that subject back on the American side of the border.

Chapter 4

River Dance

Just a few months after paddling the delta with Sam and Juan, I got a call from the National Park Service.

"Hey Pete," said a friendly voice. "Is there any chance you'd be willing to give a talk about the Colorado River at Grand Canyon National Park?"

I felt a familiar knot in my stomach. Ever since I'd published my photos from the pulse flow, the speaking invitations had been multiplying. Yes, I cared deeply about the Colorado—but a part of me was scared. If I became known as a Colorado River advocate, would people start seeing me as a single-issue crusader? Would I stop getting assignments to cover other stories in other parts of the world?

"I don't know," I said. "Which date were you hoping for?"

"Anytime in October that works for you. . . . And how about we put you up at Phantom Ranch for the night?"

The name of that place hit me like a sucker punch. Phantom Ranch. I hadn't thought about that place in years, but suddenly I was twenty-six again, racing my sister Kate up the Bright Angel Trail while our parents cheered us on from behind.

We had gone to the Grand Canyon with some family friends to float an "upper": rafting from Lees Ferry to Phantom Ranch, then hiking out on the Bright Angel Trail, some twelve miles and five thousand vertical feet to the rim. It was my first time in the Grand Canyon, and I was enchanted by the layers of geologic time we moved through as we descended deeper and deeper into the chasm. Phantom Ranch was built on the canyon floor in 1922 to serve visitors who wished to hike below the rim without needing to camp in a tent. Its stone and wood cabins are the only public lodging below the rim within the national park.

I remembered how on the drive to Lees Ferry, my dad was frantic.

"I forgot my binoculars," he said. "Laurie, do you have my vitamins? And what about that geology guide I bought for the trip?"

"Dad, it's fine," my sister and I reassured him.

"I have your binoculars, Mom has your vitamins, and whatever else you're worrying about, you won't miss," I said.

Still, he couldn't seem to relax. Even though he loved to travel, it was always hard for him to transition from work to play. In contrast, my mom was serene. She'd brought her watercolors, and the moment we set up camp on a riverbank the first afternoon, she built a makeshift easel with driftwood and began to paint.

When you go on these trips, you work your way down through layers of rock and time, slowing dropping through the Colorado Plateau and 1.2 billion years of geologic events: long-vanished seas, mass extinctions, ancient Puebloan migrations. During your descent, you start to shed layers of your own: layers of being too busy, or afraid of missing out, or needing everything to be a certain way.

My dad lived in his binoculars, clutching them to his face and studying every nook and cranny in the rocks. By the time we got to North Canyon on day three, he had completely chilled out. He'd forgotten all about the stuff he'd forgotten to pack and was sitting on the beach, shaving with a dull razor, trying to use a broken shard of something or other as a mirror. And by the time we got to Phantom Ranch, we were a regular bunch of river rats: relaxed, rumpled, and happy as clams. My sister and I ran the twelve miles to the rim, just to prove we could, while our parents and longtime family friends ambled behind.

Now, the voice on the phone urged me back to the present moment. "Pete? How 'bout it? We know you get busy, but the talk would be next year and we would love to have you."

"Of course," I said. "Count me in. I'd be honored."

~

Remembering that rafting trip with my parents and sister made me yearn to see the Grand Canyon from a boat again, so I pitched a story to *National Geographic*. When they said yes, I called up my brother.

"*Juaaaanito*," I said, dragging out my nickname for him. "How would you like to come on a dory trip with me? It would be like the one Kate and I did with Mom and Dad back in the day, but longer—all the way through Lava Falls. You'll finally be able to see the canyon."

I described the Class V rapids we'd get to paddle through. "Where do I sign up?" he said.

Johno, like me, is an action addict. After growing up playing hockey and ski racing, he went on to coach both the US national and Olympic ski teams. He married and had three children whom he and his wife Sunni were raising in a 130-year-old cabin on the ranch, surrounded by open nature and opportunities for adventure beyond the lure of screens.

I told myself that traveling down the canyon by dory would give me an intimate look at this stretch of the Colorado, now that I had the context to understand what I saw. But eleven days into our journey, as we approached Lava Falls—what many consider the most formidable rapid in the 277-mile stretch—I was questioning my own wisdom. I could hear the thunderous roar growing louder as we approached, sounding like a freight train barreling through the canyon. My hands clutched the gunwales of our dory, the *Okeechobee*, a vessel that had been rebuilt at least five times in its thirty-five years on the river.

Johno was sitting beside me in the bow. I'd always looked up to him as the solid, principled, fearless older brother—the guy who never got tired of loading hay bales or running to fix something. Right then, though, I saw nervousness in his eyes that mirrored my own. Although he lived on the front lines of high-speed, adrenaline-filled World Cup downhill ski racing, this was even wilder. The river raged before us and we were at its mercy.

"You got it, Moqui!" Johno yelled to Mark "Moqui" Johnson, the veteran boatman working the oars behind us. "You're king of the world!" Johnson had earned the "king" title after decades of navigating the Colorado's most fearsome rapids. But even the king looked intensely focused as we approached.

We dropped down a glassy green tongue at the rapid's entrance, and a wave curled over us. The dory stalled just long enough to push us sideways off our intended line. I glanced back to see our captain make a crucial corrective stroke, but then my stomach dropped: his left hand clawed the air, empty. No oar. White water thundered around us as we drifted uncontrollably toward the very heart of Lava Falls. Plan A was gone with the oar. We were left with plan B—survival.

~

Eleven days earlier, we'd set out from Lees Ferry in five dories and three baggage rafts—a group of eighteen passengers and five guides. From the moment we pushed off, I'd noticed the change in the river from what I'd seen upstream. Gone was the sediment-rich, ruddy water that had given the Colorado its name. The dam had trapped the river's red lifeblood behind concrete walls, releasing water that was unnaturally clear.

"Too thick to drink and too thin to plow," went the old description of the pre-dam Colorado. Now it looked more like a cold, clear mountain stream and less like the silt-rich red of the canyon walls—and that was a problem. The native fish who depended on warm, silty, nutrient-rich water didn't know what to make of the cold, clear stuff flowing out of the dam. Now, many of those native fish were being displaced by invasive species like small-mouth bass, which do well in warm water and eat everything.

"These beaches are smaller than I remember," I said to Andre Potochnik, a PhD geologist who was one of our main guides. "My family and I came here about twenty years ago, and I recall us playing on huge sandbars and tossing a Frisbee on long beaches."

"That's a big problem," he said. "Back when the Colorado River was wild, the floods that happened each year would have replenished its sandbars with sediment. These days, most of that sediment gets stuck in Lake Powell, and there's nothing left to build beaches or riverbanks for camping. But you want to know what the worst part is?"

I braced myself. "Go on."

"The Colorado River as it exists today—all this clear, clean water you see—wouldn't be able to carve out the Grand Canyon. For one thing, there isn't *enough* water, but it also isn't gritty enough. The river you see now couldn't have created this."

He waved at the epic canyon walls.

"A river that can't carve a canyon," I said. "That's like a painter without a brush."

He nodded sadly. "That's what happens when you think of nature in terms of dollar signs," he said. Viewed through this lens, species like the humpback chub or condors or mountain lions had no value—never mind the people who fished, worshipped, and lived around the rims.

The more I chatted with the veteran dory team, the more I understood just how different the landscape I saw before me was from the Grand Canyon as it existed before the 1950s. And I realized with dismay that there were still plenty of people who looked at the canyon's land, water, and minerals as though they were not being used economically, and ought to be converted to a "different kind" of wealth—the kind with a bunch of zeros after a positive number. For some, the idea of turning the place's beauty into cash was addictive.

Each morning, thanks to the dam, the river generally ran low, leaving our boats beached high on the sand. By midmorning the waters would usually begin to rise—a daily hydroelectric curve triggered by air conditioners in Phoenix demanding more power, causing dam operators upstream to release more water. The Colorado's pulse now followed human needs rather than natural rhythms, and it was happening right before our eyes.

It was tempting to condemn all the dams and diversions as unequivocally bad. The question that had plagued me on the delta came floating back into my head: Why is it so hard to do the right thing? Gazing at the deep canyon walls, it occurred to me that the answer—or part of it—was time. Now that the dams and reservoirs had been built, millions of people depended on them. Entire cities had sprung up that would not otherwise exist. It wasn't as simple as hitting an "undo" button and putting the ecosystem back to baseline.

The water attorney Peter Culp, who helped engineer the pulse flow downstream, once told me, "This is a civilization problem—not a river issue. The river will return one day. But our civilization built around it may not." His point made sense, but I still yearned to see a wilder element of the river—not in some distant future, but now.

On our fifth day, at river mile 68, the canyon walls suddenly spread wide, revealing both rims for the first time, looming nearly a mile above us. The sense of scale was humbling. I spotted what looked like ancient stone structures high above and couldn't resist an exploratory hike.

Forty-five minutes of scrambling brought me to ruins that had endured for nine centuries. Ancient Puebloans had farmed and lived here until abandoning the canyon for reasons still debated. Some scholars believe that severe droughts made it close to impossible to grow enough food to survive in the canyon for a span of decades. Others propose that deforestation and soil erosion contributed to the difficulty of growing enough food. Whatever the cause, the ancestral Puebloans migrated to areas with more reliable access to water, such as New Mexico's Rio Grande Valley.

Standing among their stone dwellings, I tried to imagine growing crops in this harsh environment, carrying water up from the river day after day. The silence was so complete that when a canyon wren called, it held the entire space.

The next day, my sense of timelessness was shattered by the sight of a uniquely modern invention: helicopters. Not just one,

Ancient Puebloan ruins are illuminated beneath the canyon's rim.

but sixteen of them, flying up the canyon in what appeared to be a formation. For a moment, I wondered if I was witnessing an aerial display.

"Hey Sjoden," I called to one of the guides. "What are all those helicopters doing?"

He grimaced.

"Welcome to Heli Alley," he said. "Don't worry, we'll get through this stretch as fast as we can."

"I thought helicopters weren't allowed to fly in the Grand Canyon," I shouted above the sound of whirring rotors echoing off the rocks.

"They're not," he said. "They land on the Hualapai reservation. It borders the park, but it's not technically *inside* the park."

The other guides shared Sjoden's look of disgust—like they wished they could chase the helicopters off like noisy, irritating flies.

"The tourists all come from Las Vegas," another guide explained. "They zip in, drink a glass of champagne, and zip out—all day, every day. Completely oblivious to the sound pollution they're causing for literally everyone else."

"How is that even legal in a national park that doesn't allow drones?" I asked.

"The tribe argued that they needed a way to make money. So back in the early 2000s, the FAA gave the Hualapai special dispensation to let helicopters fly and land below the rim of the canyon. Now it's one of the busiest helicopter landing sites in the world."

As we paddled on, the drone of helicopters was incessant, making the majesty of the canyon impossible to enjoy. The chatter and laughter on the dories died out, and everyone seemed to settle into a mood of grim resignation or downright crankiness. When I considered the fact that the helicopter tours hadn't existed at anywhere near this scale when I'd visited with my parents, the speed, intensity, and seeming irreversibility of the change alarmed me. Every time we authorized a new tourist activity or development project in and around the canyon, another piece of silence or stillness was gone forever. What would this place even look like in another twenty years?

~

We were approaching several major rapids created where a geological unconformity had pushed 1.8-billion-year-old granite schist to the surface. Sjoden offered a safety refresher, noting with a wry smile that we were "heading into some deep schist."

Johno and I exchanged a knowing look. We both figured out long ago that we'd rather live with a little bit of risk and face tough challenges because it makes us feel more alive than living in comfort.

With excess comfort and luxury comes boredom, isolation, and maybe even depression. I'd experienced all of those. For some people, waking up in the same cozy house each day represents the peak of happiness. For me, life without change felt like stagnation. Don't get me wrong—I loved time at home, cooking, movie nights with stormy weather, hanging out with my parents and family, coaching my nephew's hockey team, and being part of the community. But without meaningful challenges to conquer, I felt a bit like a big, playful dog who was kept on a leash. I needed to burn off my energy, or it would sour. My closest friends understood this; a long string of ex-girlfriends had not. I'd take deep schist over a pleasant and uneventful paddle any day.

The dories bobbed like corks through Granite, Hermit, and Crystal rapids, soaking us but staying upright. The boats seemed to magically correct themselves despite the churning water.

"You two want to try?" Lars, one of the boatmen, offered the oars to Johno and me during a calmer stretch. My brother went first and within minutes had us spinning sideways, then backward.

"We're going to *diiiee!*" Lars wailed dramatically, his cry echoing off canyon walls.

I took the oars next, quickly learning for myself that dories didn't forgive mistakes. One wrong stroke, and the river seized control. After twenty pulls, I thought I had the feel of it. Rounding a bend, we entered shadow, and I heard a low rumble ahead. White water. My palms began to sweat against the wooden handles.

"Want me to take over?" Lars asked.

"You've got this one," he said when I hesitated. "Satan's Jaws. No biggie."

I struggled to read the currents, following bubble lines that showed the main flow. With each stroke the river fought back. I adjusted, overcorrected, fought to keep us straight.

"Keep us alive, Pete," Johno teased from the bow.

We bucked through a series of waves and emerged intact on the other side. Only later did I learn that Lars had invented the name "Satan's Jaws" for what was actually an insignificant unnamed riffle, a practical joke at my expense.

We paused at river mile 167, camping on a beach near the mouth of National Canyon. The roar of Lava Falls carried upriver.

Sjoden announced we'd wait for the dam-released flow to rise, giving us the water we needed to navigate the formidable rapid ahead.

I was struck once again by the way we'd tamed this enormous river. I'd already seen how diversions in the Colorado affected ecosystems, from the dried-up peatlands and invasive plants in Rocky Mountain National Park to the dry delta where seeds had to wait for years for enough water to germinate. It pained me to think that even this most famously protected of areas could not be insulated from the effects of human tinkering.

"Let's go for a hike," Moqui suggested, leading us up the canyon. Within minutes we entered a labyrinth of water-smoothed Muav Limestone. The walls narrowed until we moved single file through a corridor barely wide enough for our shoulders. Then the space opened, revealing a pool of crystalline blue water beneath overhanging walls.

Johno and I locked eyes, wordlessly stripped to our shorts, and plunged in. Our laughter bounced off stone walls that had witnessed the passage of time measured in millions of years.

Returning to camp, I rounded a bend and nearly collided with an elderly man carrying bundled plants. His weathered face showed no surprise at finding strangers in this remote place. Two other men followed, similarly burdened.

I learned they were Hualapai tribe members on a spiritual journey. Each year, revenue from the river's hydroelectric operations funded trips for Navajo, Hopi, Zuni, and Hualapai people to visit sacred sites within the canyon—one of many bittersweet ironies I would encounter the better I got to know this place.

"We are blessing tobacco for our ceremonies," the elder explained when I introduced myself. "We find it wild here. The harder to find, the better for ceremonies." After a pause, he added, "Welcome to Hualapai."

I wanted to ask more about their relationship with the canyon, about how they balanced ancient traditions with modern pressures, but they were clearly on a mission. "Thank you for letting us visit your beautiful land," I said instead.

The elder looked at me sharply, then his expression softened. "I grew up there," he said, pointing with his chin to a ridge high above. "I'm used to all you coming here. I just hope you respect it."

I later learned that when the federal government established the park, they effectively redrew the map, creating boundaries that didn't align with tribal territories or traditional usage patterns. The Havasupai, in particular, were restricted to a tiny reservation of just 518 acres at the bottom of a side canyon, losing access to their traditional plateau lands where they farmed during summer months. It wasn't until 1975 that they regained some of their ancestral lands after decades of struggle.

Now, more than a century later, development pressures were mounting from all sides—a proposed 1.4-mile tramway at the Little Colorado confluence, uranium mining near the rim, helicopter tours shattering the silence, resorts and attractions proliferating. The more I learned about these proposed developments, the more urgent it felt to document the canyon. Maybe I could draw attention to the threats facing this "protected" place and help shift the needle in some small way.

When we returned to our boats, the river had risen enough to attempt Lava Falls. One by one, the other dories made clean runs through the rapid. Then it was our turn.

As we dropped into the maelstrom with one oar missing, Moqui calmly announced, "Time for plan B. Get ready . . . and . . . *hiiiigh siiiiide!*"

A massive wave was bearing down on us. When it hit, we all lunged to the highest side of the boat to counter the force. The water buried us, and we plunged into emerald darkness. All sound vanished. Everything—dory, bodies, even the roar of the rapid—submerged in slow-motion silence.

The *Okeechobee* rolled onto its side in the hydraulic jaws of Lava Falls. Somewhere in that moment of suspension between capsize and recovery, I sensed a giant grin. Johno and I sat in the front row in an overdue sibling adventure, in the heart of a river that helped shape the greatest of canyons—and much of our childhood.

The V-wave released us, pitching us sideways into the final obstacle—a standing tsunami called the Big Kahuna. Just as we seemed certain to flip, the wave let us go. Somehow we emerged upright.

"High fives!" Moqui hollered, then immediately added, "Now bail, dammit; we are *not* done." In a frantic scramble of arms, laughter, and bailing scoops, we emptied the waterlogged *Okeechobee*.

≈

That evening around a campfire on Tequila Beach, as stories and drinks flowed, everyone in our group agreed we needed more time in the canyon. We now understood how someone could come for a single trip down the Colorado and end up staying a lifetime. Looking at the faces around the fire—my brother who had shared so many adventures, the guides who had collectively taken some five hundred trips down the canyon, the other passengers who had begun as strangers and become friends—I understood why people were so passionate about this place.

"I'm so glad our parents took us to wild places like this," I said to Johno.

"I know, we're lucky," he replied. "They sure dragged us all over the place—hiking, camping, river trips. At times we didn't love it, but it sure beat growing up in front of a television."

Listening to the Colorado rushing by our campsite, I made a silent promise: I would continue doing my best to tell the river's story and advocate for its future, even if it meant signing myself up for more type-2 fun: discomfort, danger, and heartbreak. I fell asleep thinking, *Be careful what you promise, and who you promise it to*...

Chapter 5

The Call of the Canyon

A few months after going on that rafting trip with Johno, I found myself standing in front of Phantom Ranch, marveling at how well the historic buildings had stood the test of time. The night before, I'd addressed a packed audience beneath the stars, and now the ranger who had organized my visit was taking me on a hike to one of her favorite off-trail spots: the top of a little butte whose south end was etched with 110-year-old graffiti from some of the Grand Canyon's early non-native visitors before it was a national park.

"When people think about hiking in the Grand Canyon, they think about the Bright Angel Trail, maybe the Havasupai Falls trail if they're in good shape. But there's so much more to the Grand Canyon than people realize," she said. "The backcountry is incredible, and almost no one ever goes there. Believe it or not, more people have stood on the moon than thru-hiked the Grand Canyon. Isn't that wild?"

As we hiked the easy, well-worn path back to the river, I began to fantasize about spending months surrounded by red rock and warm desert light, listening to the Colorado flow through the masterpiece it had carved in its wetter, wilder, grittier days. I remembered what Andre had said about the ways we'd hobbled the river when we reduced its flows and took away its sediment. What did it mean that millions of people each year came to marvel at a thing that our thirst had depleted so starkly? Did they even realize that the river they were seeing today had so little in common with the canyon's original architect? And if they knew, what would they want to do about it? I started thinking that maybe my next project should be a walk in the park—a long one—tip to tail, end to end through the canyon. By the sounds of it, that would be an even bigger adventure than going to space.

The next day, following a leisurely breakfast at Phantom Ranch, I hiked twelve miles back to the rim, knowing that my sister was going to tease me about the fact that I had walked instead of run. When I got back to cell service, my shirt soaked in sweat and my temples throbbing from the heat, I immediately called my friend Kevin Fedarko. He lived about 80 miles away in Flagstaff, Arizona. As a lover of the canyon, an apprentice river guide, and a gifted writer, he was the perfect person to help me pull this off.

"You and I should hike the length of the Grand Canyon," I blurted out.

He began to laugh.

"Just wait," I said. "I'm getting in my car and driving to your house right now. I'll explain the whole idea when I get there."

"Pete, get a motel. You sound exhausted."

"I'm fine," I said—but after coming a little too close to nodding off behind the wheel, I pulled over on a dirt road and slept in my car beneath some ponderosa pines before resuming the drive to Kevin's the next morning.

Kevin has always been a writer, but to me he was also a trusted friend, despite the profound differences in our personalities.

I sought action and craved activity and sports; he preferred the library, quiet conversation, or silence. I was generally an optimist; he turned toward the darker side of things. Nevertheless, we had worked together as magazine journalists for years, and during our adventure assignments heyday we had developed a friendship forged through the challenges of storytelling in the remote reaches of the world—he on the written side; I on the visual.

Kevin and I have a long, complicated history of working together on stories that turn into what he calls "the equivalent of a very large boat that ran into an iceberg." We've been through a lot together, Kevin and I, and most of it has involved some level of bad luck or disaster.

On our first collaboration we set out to photograph the largest caribou migration in North America. You would think that two journalists would be capable of locating a massive herd of animals moving across the landscape—or, to quote Kevin, "the largest charismatic herd of megafauna on the North American continent." We spent three weeks out there, and all we found was one skull, which belonged to a moose. Kevin still brings that up whenever he wants to remind me of my shortcomings as a planner.

Then there was the time was in Djibouti, a small country in eastern Africa, where we went to document people selling khat, a stimulant drug. We'd entered the country with tourist visas, claiming to be scuba divers. When the authorities discovered what we were really up to, they deported us. I had to smuggle the images out, which left me with a stress-induced ulcer.

On another assignment, we attempted to document the border patrol that worked on skis in the Caucasus Mountains between Chechnya and Georgia. After one day with the patrol, we got pinned down by a seven-day storm that isolated the region with a maze of avalanches. We took shelter with truck drivers in a defunct bank, butchered a steer for food, and eventually hitchhiked back to Tbilisi, Georgia, on a helicopter hired by parsley traders. You can't make this stuff up.

But perhaps the most harrowing of our adventures was on Mount Everest. We went to document the Sherpas who build the route that allows Western climbers to summit the mountain. Nobody ever tells their stories; they're the unsung heroes of Everest, shouldering the brunt of the route-finding risk so others can climb the mountain safely. We nearly died when a massive avalanche released above us and detonated in a crevasse, showering us in clouds of ice crystals inside the Khumbu Icefall. We were lucky to make it out alive.

So yes, Kevin and I had had some debacles. But despite this rather checkered past, I had a hunch that Kevin's love for the canyon would overcome his better judgment. I already knew he was fascinated by and obsessed with this landscape, having worked in the canyon as a river guide and written an entire book about an improbable and dangerous speed run a trio of river guides had taken through the canyon during a catastrophic 1983 flood. I knew that this idea would be almost impossible for him to resist, despite our history of misadventures.

"The best part is," I told him, standing in his living room looking loopy and disheveled after sleeping in my car, "it's going to coincide with the hundred-year anniversary of the founding of the National Park Service. The timing could not be more perfect."

I caught my breath. "Actually, that's not the best part," I said. "The best part is, this fits in *perfectly* with all the projects I've been doing about the Colorado—and I happen to know that you're just as obsessed with that river as I am."

He gave me a rueful look. It was clear I'd piqued his interest, against his better judgment.

"Pete," he said, "do you have any idea how *hot* the canyon gets? Do you realize how hard it is to find *water*? There's a reason people don't do this. Especially people like us."

"Of course I know how hot it gets," I assured him. "I just did a dory trip with Johno. We nearly melted, almost flipped, and loved every second."

Kevin leaned back in his chair, pinching the bridge of his nose.

"Pete, I need you to understand what we're actually talking about here," he said, his voice carrying that patient tone I'd heard countless times before—the one that meant I was being dense about something obvious. "People hear the word 'thru-hike' and they think of the Pacific Crest Trail (PCT) or the Appalachian Trail (AT)—a well-marked path, with guidebooks and maps and even apps to help you find campsites and water. A trail that literally thousands of people do every year."

"Exactly," I said. "And guess what—those trails are over two thousand miles each. The Grand Canyon is only 277 miles."

"No, not exactly," Kevin said, reaching for a topographic map. "Look at this. In the Grand Canyon, you're not just walking horizontally. For every mile you cover as the crow flies, you climb up and down thousands of vertical feet—multiple times. We'll be walking more like six or seven hundred miles—the length of California—and the elevation gain and loss is going to be insane. With all the up and down to find a route, we'd be going up or down three, four, or five thousand feet a day. All said, we would climb some one hundred thousand vertical feet or more, easily. And just to refresh your memory, Mount Everest is twenty-nine thousand feet."

I shrugged. "We're in good shape. And we have backcountry experience . . . compared to the average bear, I mean. Just think of all the adventures we've already done—really challenging stuff. It's not like we're a couple of couch potatoes."

I eyed his sofa in the corner. "I figure I can train by climbing mountains around Basalt, and you can train by . . . " I waved my hand at the desert landscape outside his living room window. "You know. Doing some hard hikes around here in the San Francisco Peaks. Point is, we'll train."

Kevin ignored me. "You know we can't just stick to the river, right? As I'm sure you noticed on your dory trip, the river is cliffed out for long stretches; and even when it's not cliffed out, we'd be bushwhacking through tamarisk for days at a time. There wouldn't be anything to photograph or write about except thorns. For this to be worth it, we'd have to hike up into the hinterlands of the canyons, the ledges and alcoves, but that means hunting for water. . . . Every. Single. Day."

"Le duh," I said. "But look, many springs are marked on the map, others we can research, and at times we'd have to slop back to the river. Sure, it's going to take some planning, but it's not impossible."

He cradled his head in his hands. "You realize this is probably the hardest hike on the planet, right?"

I grinned. "That's why it's going to make a great story. And for the record, it's not like we're flying totally blind here. I've already got another dory trip in the works so I can scout locations for our food caches and record the GPS coordinates. I can pitch it to Sadie at *National Geographic* and round up sponsorships for gear. And I've already contacted a canyon guru badass who's going to teach us how to survive down there and show us the way through Marble Canyon. The best part—the reason you can't say no—is that this walk will give us a framework for looking at things like mining, overdevelopment, and water use in and around the canyon. All you need to do is show up."

Dare I say that Kevin looked the slightest bit impressed? "OK," he sighed. "I could be in."

―――

Although Kevin likes to play up my happy-go-lucky nature for comedic effect, the truth is that even I knew we wouldn't stand a chance in the canyon without an expert to teach us how to survive. Luckily, I knew just the person to help us. A few years earlier, a friend of mine had introduced me to Rich Rudow, who may be the most seasoned Grand Canyon hiker on the planet.

"Rich has logged more time hiking in the Grand Canyon than probably anyone else alive today," my friend explained. I was expecting a grizzled character along the lines of Edward Abbey or Martin Litton—the river runner and environmental activist who led the fight against the Marble Canyon Dam—and was caught off guard when he led me up to an unassuming balding guy in his late forties who enthusiastically shook my hand.

I later learned that Rich had led over one hundred technical first descents of slot canyons in the Grand Canyon and completed sixteen river trips, most of them in the winter. Clearly, this guy was a total beast—but you wouldn't hear him bragging about it. When

I first met him, waiting in line at the Telluride Film Festival in September of 2012, he looked like a mild-mannered high school chemistry teacher who ran half-marathons in his spare time.

Recently, I'd gotten wind that Rich was putting together a team of highly experienced long-distance hikers to thru-hike the canyon with him. Maybe Kevin and I could tag along—not for the whole thing, of course, but just for the first few days, enough to get the hang of things. Once we'd gotten our sea legs, Rich and his team could blast off ahead of us, and we could finish the rest of the hike at our own pace, with breaks between each section.

When I called up Rich and explained the mission—to document the Grand Canyon in all four seasons, with a focus on the threats from tourist development and uranium mining pressure, as well as my ongoing interest in dams and drought—he agreed to let us join his party for the first twelve days, which would see us through one of the most challenging sections of the canyon.

Kevin and I had no intention of joining Rich's team—their plan relied on extreme speed and agility, which would have left no time for taking photographs, shooting video, or taking notes—but the truth is, we wouldn't have been remotely qualified even if we had wanted to. Although Kevin and I were far more fit and experienced than the average person, the Grand Canyon required a whole different level of preparation, skill, and self-discipline. The lackadaisical "just keep putting your head down and it will all work out" attitude I tended to fall back on had little place in a canyon where dying of thirst was a daily risk.

"Good news," I reported back to Kevin. "Rich and his guys are going to show us the ropes. By the time we part ways with them, we'll be canyon-crunching machines."

"OK, Pete," he replied. "I'm in, but that sounds rather optimistic."

―

A year after the trip with Johno, I joined another dory trip. A river rafting outfitter called OARS had hired me to make a documentary about the first run of a special new dory called the *Marble Canyon*, built in honor of Martin Litton. When time allowed, I could also do some scouting for the thru-hike.

It felt amazing to be back on the river. And this time, I got to row my own film boat, trading off rapids with my film team—JP Clark, a guide and gear guru, and Blake McCord, a fellow cinematographer and adventure lover. As the captain of our baggage raft, I got to pick my three favorite rapids—Hance, Hermit, and Lava.

Now that I was familiar with some of the beaches, rapids, and other landmarks, the canyon was starting to feel like home. As we floated past red rock, I counted miles. Kevin and I would need to have a food stash about every forty miles, but some forty-mile markers were more accessible than others. Theoretically, it would be possible to do this work from home, using a map, but from a boat it was much easier to imagine how hard it would be for us to access each stash. Peering up at the canyon walls, I'd think, *Alright, we'll probably be up on that ledge, a thousand feet above the river there, but we could get down to this spot. So let's leave a cache here and keep it away from camps and potential mice.*

I carefully recorded the GPS coordinates for each future stash spot. I knew that being able to find those precious buckets of supplies was going to be crucial, especially since Kevin and I would already be eating less food than our bodies needed each day. I definitely didn't want us to be stumbling around in the baking sun, digging in the hot rocks for a bucket of food we couldn't find.

When I wasn't hunting for stash spots, I soaked in the stories people shared about Martin Litton. Like my dad, Litton had been trained as a pilot during his military service, and when he returned to civilian life he continued to fly a Cessna. When he saw Lake Powell from the air, the scope of the destruction blew his mind. He realized what would be lost if Marble Canyon met a similar fate—and devoted himself to stopping the dam that was being proposed there.

In a time before aerial photography was commonplace, getting a bird's-eye view of a landscape was a big deal. Few people had the perspective to see the true impact of dams on a river system. Litton did.

When he started a river rafting business in the Grand Canyon, he named each of his dories after places in nature that had been destroyed or come close to being destroyed. He rowed many dory trips himself, becoming famous for taking some of the hardest lines and "letting the river figure it out."

Kevin had once ridden through Lava Falls with Martin, then age eighty-eight, at the oars. It would be Martin's last run—and like so many runs before, he didn't flip.

As I listened to the river guides reminiscing about Martin's larger-than-life role in the American conservation movement, I couldn't help but reflect on the way my own environmental consciousness had been awakened by those flights I'd taken over the Colorado River with my dad. Sure, I'd always cared about the environment, but it wasn't until I saw the dams, canals, sprawling suburbs, and tailing ponds from the sky that I really started to understand what was going on, or make it my mission to show others. Seeing the scale of the alterations to the river's natural flow had helped me understand the stakes in a way that reading US Geological Survey reports never could, no matter how well-researched or carefully illustrated they were.

I felt a twinge of wistfulness when I contemplated Litton's accomplishments, which were so visible and easy to measure. Would I ever be able to raft through a river canyon and think, *This place would be a hundred feet underwater if not for me?* Would I ever look at a lush green delta and be able to say, *This was dried up and abandoned until my advocacy work inspired people to save it?* I had a feeling the answer was no. It seemed to me the era of the lone environmental hero had come and gone, not to mention the era when a single film or photograph could spark a movement. But maybe that meant something new was taking its place: native and non-native communities standing up for their local waterways and getting credit for it, instead of romanticizing a single individual who was all too often bearded and white.

In the years since I'd started documenting the Colorado River, people sometimes asked me if I saw myself as an activist. It was becoming more and more clear to me that the answer was no. I didn't want to be boxed into a role others created. I just wanted to be a witness to water, and a visual voice for the people and places most affected by our decisions about water. I wanted to use my camera to amplify the unsung efforts of those who were doing the real work—the activists and community members whose collective effort over years and decades was making a difference for our wild places. I wanted to give a voice to the voiceless, be they wild critters or the rivers themselves.

With my scouting mission complete, I moved on to the next step in our preparations: wrangling permits from the National Park Service, which wasn't thrilled about the prospect of anyone wandering around the park outside of established trails, let alone a couple of relative canyon newbies like Kevin and me. We spent hours poring over maps, noting the location of seeps, springs, and potholes where we might have a chance of finding water, and created detailed itineraries based on this information, knowing that we could only carry enough water for one day at a time.

Food and fuel presented another challenge. With no regular resupply points such as those you'd find on established trails like the PCT or the AT, we had to coordinate with friends who would help place our food caches at the points I'd identified along the river, and collect the empty buckets once we'd used them. Our caches would need to be in animal-proof containers, and covered in dire warnings for any curious humans who might stumble upon them: DO NOT TAKE. LIFE OR DEATH DEPENDS ON THIS.

Perhaps equally important, we had to prepare our partners and families for the fact that we would be more or less incommunicado anytime we were below the rim. Kevin and his girlfriend had already been struggling, and she wasn't pleased that he was abandoning her yet again to risk his life in some far-flung place with a bozo like me. As for me, I'd recently started dating a fun, lighthearted Brazilian woman. Luckily for me, the mystique of dating an adventure photographer had yet to wear off. Still, I worried that it would only be a matter of time until she started wondering why I was paying more attention to topo maps than I was to her.

Once we entered the canyon, we would be in some of the remotest landscapes on earth—if not as the crow flies, then in terms of access to rescue. Every year, an average of fifteen people die in the Grand Canyon—most from heat-related illness, but some from drowning or falling—and the majority of those deaths represent people hiking or rafting in well-traveled sections of the park, where there's at least some hope of rescue. Kevin and I would be moving through places where humans rarely set foot at all.

I wasn't that worried, though. Kevin and I were resilient and levelheaded in the field . . . *generally*. God knew we'd gotten ourselves out of enough scrapes over the course of our professional relationship. No matter what the canyon threw at us, I was confident we could handle it. Besides, we would have Rich and his team with us for the first, toughest, leg of the journey.

On the night before I left for Arizona, I had dinner with my parents.

"You know, Pete," said my dad, "when normal guys have a midlife crisis, they buy a sports car."

"Oh *Johnnnnnnny*, who are you to joke about a midlife crisis?" said my mom. "What do you call that thing sitting out there in the hangar?"

"I've been flying since I was fourteen—long before any midlife crisis," he said. They both laughed.

"You guys, this is a serious project," I said. "Nobody realizes how many threats the canyon is facing. Kevin and I could help move the needle with public awareness."

"We know, Peto," said my mom, reaching across the table to pat my hand. "We were just joking. If we were a little younger, we'd want to join you."

Chapter 6

A Canyon in the Crosshairs

Kevin and I took the first steps of our Grand Canyon hike on a quiet morning in late September. We trailed behind Rich and his crew, trying our best to keep up with them as they wriggled through tamarisk thickets and rock-hopped through fields of boulders. The speed they were moving, you'd think we were trying to make it to the world's most killer taqueria before it closed.

"Kevin," I whispered, "why are they walking so fast? What's the rush?"

"Dude, they're on a schedule," he said, "and we already made them late when we weren't ready to go this morning. They're not going to slow down."

We'd gone barely five miles when I started to struggle. My shirt was soaked in sweat, and the fifty-five-pound pack I'd stuffed with extra camera lenses weighed me down with every step. When we finally staggered into camp at sunset, ten hours after starting our hike, I realized I'd barely taken a single photo all day.

"Kevin," I said, "if we keep this pace with these dudes for twelve more days, I'm not sure I'll make a single photo. They are hauling ass—it almost feels like they're racing."

"You should have known that when you signed us up for this," he said. "Pete, we're *screwed*."

That night, I curled up in a guilty ball and fell asleep, hoping tomorrow would somehow bring mercy.

～

The next day did not bring mercy—or the next day, or the next. By day six, Kevin's feet were encased in blisters, and I had cramps running through my entire body. At one point, my cramping got so bad that my forearms and fingers locked in talon-like positions. Even my tongue cramped. When the cramping moved to my stomach muscles, it looked like something was squirming around under my skin. Later, Kevin would describe it as a mouse snacking on my intestines. The heat turned the canyon walls into a shimmering hallucination. I could barely hold my camera, let alone compose a shot. My vision shrank, and I sensed I was on the verge of unconsciousness.

Even though I knew going into this that we weren't going to be walking next to the river, I still wasn't mentally prepared for just how scary it was to move through a landscape with no guaranteed sources of water. Up until that point, most of my memories of the Grand Canyon involved water, and lots of it—blasting through rapids with Johno, tossing a Frisbee on a beach while my mom painted nearby. For all my world travels, I'd never spent much time in an environment where water was as scarce as it was here. I hadn't known what it felt like to not know where your next drop was coming from—to be thinking about water while your brain baked like a pizza in the heat.

"I need to stop for a second," I told Kevin, collapsing onto a ledge in the blazing sun. "I'll catch up with you guys."

What the heck *was* this? I'd been drinking water, even though the sun had warmed it to an unappealing bathtub temperature and then even hotter. One afternoon, my thermometer read 112 degrees Fahrenheit. That night it cooled down to a sweltering 106. I assessed my condition as dehydration based on the dark yellow-orange hue of my urine, a color my brother would often describe as "Dijon mustard." But I also felt oddly sloshy and bloated. Did I have heat stroke? Or something else?

In my years as an adventure photographer, I'd climbed thin-aired peaks, bushwhacked for miles, waded down piranha-infested rivers, scuba dived into icy blackness, and faced countless fears, many heightened thanks to my vivid imagination. But nothing compared to the sense of confusion and powerlessness that overcame me in that moment. I felt so weak it reminded me of being at high altitude on Everest, somewhere above twenty thousand feet, gasping for oxygen. But I was at a *lower* elevation than my home in Colorado. Something was very wrong with me. I was checking out. Gazing up at the white-hot sky, I thought of the statistics I'd read about deaths in the Grand Canyon. *Holy crap*, I thought, *I am that guy, soon to become a statistic.*

That night, Rich explained what was wrong with me. After texting my symptoms to a Grand Canyon doctor and friend twenty-four hours earlier, he finally got word back on his satellite device. "You might have hyponatremia," he said. "That means you have dangerously low electrolyte levels from drinking too much water compared to your salt intake. You're sweating out too many electrolytes."

I was too tired for the strange new word to sink in. *Hypo-what?* People died of dehydration in the canyon—not from lack of salt. Right?

Looking back on this hazy time, I can't help but see a parallel to the river. Like my body, the Colorado was out of whack: there was too much demand, not enough supply, and the problem had already grown too serious for the resources we had on hand to solve it. The more I sweated, the more I felt like a soda cup with too many straws in it, my life force draining out of me with every sunblasted step.

Over the next two days, I staggered along, barely conscious of the dramatic landscape, stalked by a feeling that was utterly unfamiliar to me: despair. My whole life, I'd relied on my natural buoyancy and positive attitude to carry me through. Sure, things could get rough sometimes—but I'd always found a way through with humor, determination, and a lucky break here and there. The fact that I was a fit lifelong athlete didn't hurt, either. As my hockey coach, my dad had always taught me to push through mental blocks and embrace physical challenges. "Skate it off, Pete," he'd shout from the stands when I got hit hard. "You're fine." My can-do attitude had allowed me to do some challenging things in my life. For the first time, it seemed like it might be failing me. I was *far* from fine.

≈

It was clear to everyone on Rich's team that Kevin and I needed help and would have to exit. Using his satellite communication device, Rich arranged for my friend JP Clark to hike down to a rendezvous point and help Kevin and me hike out while Rich's group carried on. When Rich informed us of the plan, I was too sick to register any relief. The cramping in my stomach had become so intense I could only stand up for a few minutes at a time.

So this was what all those dire warnings from the National Park Service were about. This was the whole reason they didn't want to give us permits in the first place. The canyon respected no one, and it didn't give any breaks. We could control the Colorado River with dams, but there was no taming the canyon it had carved in its wilder days, or the sun that pegged the temperature well over 100 degrees. And it was only getting hotter and drier, noticed hourly by us but also documented in decades of scientific data.

As I was losing myself in these ruminations, Rich appeared like an angel of mercy. He had found some soy sauce packets in his pack, which he ripped open and made me drink. The infusion of life-giving salt into my bloodstream gave me just enough strength to push on for another few miles.

~

The next day, Kevin and I followed JP 2,200 vertical feet up an ancestral Puebloan route at South Canyon. Until that moment, I hadn't fully grasped just how brutal and complicated it is to make an emergency exit from the Grand Canyon. This wasn't some quick helicopter rescue. Our movements were slow and agonizing, walking and crawling in the punishing sun, our feet swollen with infected blisters. I couldn't believe this was how the first leg of our Grand Canyon journey was ending.

When we finally reached the rim, my legs were shaking and my vision was blurry. To add more injury to injury, I'd stepped on a cactus, which shot painful spines into my right ankle. Later, the spines would become infected and need to be surgically removed. Kevin brought me to see the doctor who'd texted with Rich. After I described my cramps and tunnel vision, he confirmed I had severe hyponatremia. He gravely informed us that if we'd stayed in the canyon even a few hours longer, I would have had a seizure—at which point I would have needed an intravenous saline treatment, not easy to find in the canyon, to save my life.

I stared at the ceiling, realizing just how close I'd come to becoming a cautionary tale. As Kevin and I walked out, I turned to him. "I can't believe I'm saying this, but maybe we should call it quits."

⁓

The week after Kevin and I made our emergency exit from the canyon was one of the darkest times in my life. My debt of gratitude to Rich and his friends was thickly layered with shame. How could I ever show my face around those guys after what had happened? Who would ever trust me to take on a big assignment? The unofficial motto for *National Geographic* is "We don't publish excuses." How would I possibly explain just how impossible this assignment was?

In addition to the trek falling apart, our personal lives were taking a hit, too. Kevin's girlfriend broke up with him within hours of his return. My own relationship wasn't faring much better. That mystique I mentioned earlier was beginning to wear off. The limping, foggy-headed, whimpering shadow of a soul who emerged from the canyon with his tail between his legs didn't line up with my girlfriend's image of the invincible adventure photographer.

A few days later, with permission, I car camped alone on the Navajo grazing allotment near the canyon. I'd hoped I could get back on the story by making images of the land and people who know the canyon better than most—the Native communities who resided there for generations, long before it was a national park.

An infected heel blister made me limp when I walked, but my blurry head started to clear. A week later, I returned to Colorado to reassess. There, I walked short stretches of the headwater creeks and rivers near my home—enjoying the fresh air and sound of accessible water like a tonic. Slowly, my wounds started to mend.

Ten days later, I called up Kevin from my backyard garden shed, which I'd turned into an office.

"Hey cactus blossom," I said, using one of the nicknames we'd come up with for each other on the trail. "You're probably going to kill me for even suggesting this, but—"

"I know," he said immediately. "We need to get back to the canyon."

"Yup, but we need to rethink this whole thing. And we need a shit ton of help."

~

When my friends realized that Kevin and I were already plotting a way to get back into the canyon, when our injuries from the first trip had barely begun to heal, some of them applauded the bounce-back attitude. Others were downright annoyed.

"You almost *died*," one friend said. "You're in even worse shape than when you first started out. Why not put it off for a year? Give yourself time to get the proper training—training in the actual canyon, not climbing random mountains in Colorado."

I gave her my most convincing excuses: The permits I'd worked so hard to get would expire. Our assignment from *National Geographic* tied in with the centennial of the National Park Service, and it wouldn't be the centennial next year. You had to get back on the horse quickly after a setback, before fear had a chance to establish itself in your mind—I'd learned that one from my dad years ago at hockey practice.

But anyone who knows me well knows there's more to it than that. I loved challenges and was addicted to the process of attacking them. Life without a few audacious goals felt boring compared to the physical and psychological hurdles of being out on assignment in a little-traveled place. Getting off the couch wasn't a problem for me—it was staying *on* the couch for too long that I found difficult.

To Kevin's and my surprise, Rich had already sent out a message to the Grand Canyon hiking community asking if anyone would be willing to pick up where he and his team had left off. Within days, several canyon lovers had offered to help us get back in the saddle. They assured us that cutting down our pack weight and optimizing our nutrition would give us a fighting chance. It was decided that we would resume our hike just three weeks after JP had rescued us from South Canyon.

For our second attempt, Kevin and I returned to the canyon with two veteran canyon rats, Mathieu Brown and Kelly McGrath. This time, I cut my pack weight down to thirty-seven pounds (with two liters of water, not the full capacity plan of five), loaded my powdered meals with extra protein and fat, and left my extra camera lenses behind.

Having a lighter pack made all the difference. We moved roughly twelve to fourteen miles a day, weaving our way atop the Redwall, a layer of limestone where industrial debris from the Marble Canyon Dam exploration site quietly petrified some twelve hundred feet above the river. The Colorado looked so powerful from up there; it was hard to square this wild sight with the tamed and trapped water I'd seen backed up in reservoirs downstream.

Gazing over the canyon, I gave a silent thank-you to Martin Litton and others who had fought to stop the dam. It was a stark reminder of how quickly conservation views and values could change.

In America, we love to think of the national park system as our best idea. Rangers at Grand Canyon National Park tell the story of how Teddy Roosevelt stood on the south rim of the Grand Canyon in 1903, declaring: "Leave it as it is. You cannot improve on it. The ages have been at work on it, and man can only mar it."

The American narrative celebrates Roosevelt's conservation vision, but there's another story that's often left untold—the story of the Native peoples who were here long before any national park existed. The Havasupai have lived in and around the canyon for at least eight hundred years, relying on the river's natural flooding cycles to grow maize, beans, and squash on the fertile floodplains. The Hualapai, Navajo, Hopi, Zuni, and other tribes all have deep connections to this landscape. For them, this wasn't wilderness—the river and its canyon walls were home, hunting ground, farmland, and sacred spaces.

As we made our way along the sharp textured Redwall, we passed ancient granaries tucked into alcoves, pictographs on rock walls, and stone structures that had withstood nine hundred years of storms. These weren't relics of some mysterious vanished people—they were the handiwork of the ancestors of the same tribes still fighting for their rights to this land today. I was used to thinking of national parks as collective treasures that benefited all while harming none; now, I felt a prick of guilt as I considered what the original peoples of this place had been forced to give up so that people like me and Kevin could enjoy it.

～

By early November, we reached the confluence. The Hopi, Zuni, and Navajo tribes, among others, believe this location, where the emerald waters of the Colorado River meet the turquoise flow of the Little Colorado, marks the point where life began.

The confluence was also the site of recent conflict. Developers were looking to install a building complex on the eastern rim with a tram called the Grand Canyon Escalade, which could carry up to ten thousand people a day from the rim above to the sacred mixing waters below. In light of the fact that river trips through the canyon were limited to about twenty-six thousand people per *year*, the gondola would eclipse the annual visitation to the site in just three days. It was the first among a group of proposed developments that were threatening to change this part of the canyon forever.

The Grand Canyon Trust had arranged for us to meet with some women from an organization called Save the Confluence that was opposing the Escalade project. We left the boundary of the national park just beyond the confluence and hiked to the rim, where we were met by a group of Navajo elders, mostly women. Many had spent their entire lives there raising sheep. For most of them, Navajo was their first and only language. We were introduced to Renae Yellowhorse, who wore a red velveteen dress and moccasins. Over homemade mutton stew on the flat, brushy world above the canyon, Renae told us they didn't want to see Disneyland at the rim of their church.

"Our own Navajo Nation has the power to protect it," she told me. "They have the power to preserve it. And that's why they need to act—for the elders and for the generations to come."

The company behind the proposed development was Scottsdale-based Confluence Partners, LLC. When I later interviewed its managing partner, a non-native from Phoenix named Lamar Whitmer, he claimed that the Grand Canyon Escalade project would not only bring jobs to the economically depressed Navajo community but also give people equal access to the canyon, regardless of their physical abilities or health. He painted the Escalade's detractors as elitists who wished to keep the canyon floor all to themselves. "I think everybody's entitled to have a Grand Canyon experience, whether it's on a mule or hiking or on a helicopter," he said. "And so we're trying to offer the average person that below-the-rim experience."

Listening to Whitmer's spin, it was hard not to express my skepticism at this supposed altruistic angle. Since the project was on Navajo land, he partnered with the former president of the Navajo Nation and other Native businessmen who lived far from the canyon. With stories of deep pockets and Native partnerships, many feared the tram project would fast-track. But when I told Grand Canyon National Park superintendent David Uberuaga what Whitmer had said, he sighed in exasperation. "The average out-of-shape person *knows* they're never going to summit Everest. They're never going to be out in the middle of the ocean in a kayak. We can't provide every single experience to every single person based on their own individual abilities," he said.

Although Whitmer promised that the hotels and restaurants that would spring up around the tramway would help boost the troubled Navajo economy, the Save the Confluence women raised a host of objections. These ranged from security and light pollution to freshwater access, crowding, and cultural appropriation. If built, the silence and remoteness that characterized this sacred site would never be the same again. To top it all off, the thought of building the infrastructure to host thousands of tourists (and wash millions of sheets and towels and dishes for them, and provide water for their baths and showers) when local residents were already in dire straits for clean water just didn't add up.

Squeezed into a booth at Denny's, which served as their monthly meeting place, one of them told me, "We understand economic growth; just not here."

I realized the tram wasn't a singular issue—rather, it was related to *everything* happening around the park. It felt like vultures were circling the Grand Canyon, vying to see how much profit they could skim off. And while the various tribes stood to gain from development in some ways, it was outside corporations who would really be making a killing—a story that has been playing out in America's wild places again and again and again.

～

Kevin's seventy-six-year-old father was undergoing treatment for prostate cancer, and Kevin needed to fly to Pittsburgh to be with him. This presented us with a conundrum: For our canyon plans to work out, we had to take advantage of the relatively cool weather to push ahead. We decided that I would hike the next section of the canyon alone. After all, it featured something the previous sections did not: a trail.

I'd gotten so used to having Kevin around to talk to, tease, and annoy that walking alone came as a shock to my system. At one point, I stepped on what I was certain was a snake. It squished and slithered in surprise, and I leapt straight skyward, so startled that my sunglasses flew off my head (something I wouldn't notice until it was too late to retrieve them). Luckily, I had packed an extra pair, as ultraviolet eye protection is crucial in the harsh desert light.

I hiked the ancient Hopi salt trail that descends into the steep Little Colorado canyon. This ancient route, about ten miles south of the proposed tram site, was historically used by young Hopi and Navajo men to prove their worth. They would enter the canyon on a mission to return with pounds and pounds of salt they harvested from a seep near the river.

After a full day of frequently losing the trail and bushwhacking, I stopped a few miles above the confluence where I had been told of a freshwater spring. Unfortunately, a rancid smell in the water suggested it was too mineralized or polluted to drink. As I searched for alternate sources, I had to use every psychological skill I possessed to keep from panicking. At one point, it felt like the walls were closing in on me, squeezing out any wonder and replacing it with fear and loneliness. I thought of the saying commonly attributed to Ben Franklin, "When the well's dry, we know the worth of water."

As I trudged along, I wondered if my friends were right. Maybe I was addicted to extremes, and that addiction would someday catch up with me—or already had. Yes, I loved the camaraderie and adventure that went along with photography, and I'd found new meaning in advocating for the river, but there was more to it than that.

Photography was my job. After doing it for so long, the prospect of working a job without risk and adventure felt scarier than rattlesnakes. My restless soul had carved out the canyon of my life, and I didn't regret one moment of it, but as I hiked alone in the hot sun, I wondered just how much more I would sacrifice to keep that restlessness satisfied.

I was relieved four days later when I met my old friend Blake McCord on the trail. Blake had filmed with me on my last dory project. He brought in fresh camera batteries and some food for the hot, dusty final two days before we reached Havasupai Gardens and Phantom Ranch. There I dug into a delicious home-cooked, high-calorie meal and gave an evening talk about my adventures to forty-plus campers and park service members. The next morning, Blake and I would exit the canyon on the well-traveled Bright Angel Trail—and drop in on Kevin just in time for Thanksgiving.

Kevin's dad wasn't doing well, and his now-frequent trips to Pittsburgh meant that we couldn't begin the next leg of our hike until mid-January. I took advantage of the long break to spend time with my own family, regaling my parents with stories of my brushes with death over Christmas dinner.

By that point, my girlfriend had broken up with me, too, having grown tired of playing second fiddle to a giant hole in the ground. I couldn't blame her. I was obsessed with the canyon, and that obsession didn't leave much space for other relationships. Communicating via unreliable 120-character satellite texts didn't help. Kevin and I would return to the canyon as two forty-something single dudes—and in our sweat-stained T-shirts, we weren't exactly the picture of the world's most eligible bachelors. Of course, many before us had called the canyon their mistress. I guess it was just our turn to officially give in to her siren-like allure.

We started the next section of our hike from the Grand Canyon National Park headquarters, following the western section of the Tonto Trail. It wasn't long before we stumbled across Horn Creek, a burbling rivulet that made my soul jump for joy.

"Jackpot," I said, hurrying to unscrew the lid on my bottle. "We're going to drink like *kings* today."

"Not so fast," Kevin said. "Don't you see that sign?"

Sure enough, a small white placard read:

DANGER: RADIATION. DO NOT DRINK.

A sign warns of high radiation levels due to uranium mining.

"Oh," I said, dropping the arm that held the bottle. "The park superintendent warned me about this creek. I guess the uranium contamination is above EPA standards."

To be moving through the heart of the crown jewel of America's national park system and arrive at a spring that you can't drink from because it's radioactive is bizarre. I later learned that much of that contamination originates from the Orphan Mine on and below the southern rim next to the park headquarters. Opened in 1893 to mine copper, the mine officially started producing uranium in 1951. After closing in the late 1960s, the mine was mostly reclaimed—but not the water below it. In 1995, a research team found uranium levels in Horn Creek and fifteen other springs to be above EPA drinking water standards. Spurred by the fear of further water contamination, the federal government put new uranium exploration around the park under a twenty-year moratorium in 2012. However, existing mining operations were grandfathered in to continue business as usual, and at the time of our hike the mining industry was lobbying to lift the ban.

As Kevin and I hiked on, we tried not to think about the possible contamination we were exposing our bodies to as we drank water from the springs. I couldn't believe we had to choose between dying of thirst and glowing in the dark.

⸻

A week later, Rich Rudow, Kelly McGrath, and a former park ranger named Amy joined us as we approached the Great Thumb Mesa, a giant geologic digit that forms a twenty-mile arc north. There are few exits or breaks in the rim there, meaning that if anything went wrong, we could be in real trouble. As we pushed toward the tip of the thumb, an angry mass of dark clouds filled our view. Rain began to blast the crimson rocks, then turned to snow. For the next twenty-four hours, fluffy flakes filled our world while temperatures plummeted. This was not completely unheard of for mid-January in the canyon, but below-freezing temps, inadequate food supplies, and ice accumulation on the cliff edges made hiking in these conditions extremely risky.

"When do we call the rescue?" Kevin joked. "Now?"

But we all knew rescue wasn't an option. Even if a helicopter could have landed near the cliffs where we were perched, the snowy whiteout prevented it.

Nevertheless, the photographer in me was thrilled to see this world of red and brown and pink suddenly framed with white. Negative space took over. I kept taking off my gloves to shoot photos until a sudden gust of wind blew one of them away. I watched it flutter into the abyss of the canyon below, dancing amid the snow and fog.

Two days later, Amy dislocated her kneecap while hiking ahead of us and reduced it back into place herself. We distributed her load among ourselves to ease her travel, but she was still in serious pain with every step. Even then, a helicopter rescue seemed nearly impossible—not that Amy would have let us call one in. Her grit and determination reminded me that the canyon was no place for the weak-willed. When you were out there, you had to be able to keep going, no matter what.

Thanks to the snow, we had fallen two days behind schedule, which meant that running out of food was a real possibility. By the time we reached our next cache at the bottom of Olo Canyon, we had precisely four jelly beans left between us. It was remarkable how giddy and elated the smallest sustenance could make you feel when you were starving. Our hoots and squeals of joy at finding the food bucket reminded me of the way the people in Mexico had celebrated to see a trickle of water running down a riverbed that used to flow freely and abundantly. It was clear that in the Colorado River system, scarcity had become the defining experience—whether you were talking about clean water, uninterrupted silence, or wild nature. These days, we were all living on rations, whether or not we realized it. I wondered if it would take the taps to stop running for people to finally understand just how rationed the river really is.

On our next break between hiking segments, Kevin and I met a Havasupai leader named Carletta Tilousi. She and some of her family and youth from the community had come to the south rim to perform traditional dances at one of their sacred landscapes and protest a uranium mine about seven miles south of Grand Canyon National Park. Born and raised in Supai, a small village at the floor of the Grand Canyon—the only place in the United States where mail is still delivered by mule—Carletta had been working on the uranium mining issue since she was a teenager in the 1980s.

"Our entire water supply comes from Havasu Creek, which is fed by springs from the aquifer," she said, pointing to a blue-green ribbon visible in the distance. "If uranium contaminates that aquifer, there's no cleaning it up. Our people would have to leave. Where would we go? This has been our home since the beginning."

Carletta explained that water in the canyon traveled through layers of rock, meandering laterally and vertically through cracks, crevasses, and caves. "Some of the softer geological layers soak up water like a sponge," she told me. "But eventually, it all comes out in the canyon, bubbling up in a spring or dripping out in a seep as it tries to reach the Colorado River."

The toxic spring I'd experienced as a temporary inconvenience was, for the Havasupai, an existential threat.

Carletta told me that a park hydrologist named Benjamin Tobin had once placed fluorescent dye in sinkholes scattered on the Kaibab Plateau on the north rim. Researchers later checked the springs and creeks to see where the dye emerged. One seep, located on the north rim to the east of where we started hiking, surprised everyone.

Based on prior research, experts assumed the colored dye would flow downstream. Instead, it traveled twenty-four horizontal miles and dropped six thousand vertical feet. Traces of the dye showed up in a series of springs, including Vasey's Paradise in Marble Canyon to the east, and Deer Creek, Thunder River, and Tapeats Creek over a hundred miles to the west.

"It's all connected," Carletta said.

I blinked, suddenly understanding that every drop of water Kevin and I had found or struggled to find was connected to a complex system much larger than we could see. The canyon wasn't just teaching us about survival; it was showing us how our actions in one place could profoundly affect the environment many miles away. This suggested that containing pollution was much harder than extractive industries like uranium mining wanted us to believe.

Listening to Carletta talk, I remembered all the other communities I'd visited along the river—from ranchers in Colorado to farmers in the Imperial Valley to cowboys in Mexico. Although all those people didn't necessarily think of themselves as being connected, their decisions impacted each other in ways they didn't always realize, often across hundreds of miles. Restoring the river would mean learning to not only consider the impacts we can't see with our own eyes, but to care deeply about the people downstream.

Later that afternoon Carletta, her daughter Maya, and other members of their community brought their drums, dances, and protest songs to the entrance of Canyon Mine. Wearing traditional clothes, including colorful ankle-length skirts and beaded jewelry, they sang and danced just beyond the mine's chain-link fence.

Havasupai tribal members protest in front of Canyon Mine.

"Our job as Havasupai is to keep our culture and keep our songs, because that's all we have left as Indigenous people," she said, gesturing at the dancers and the drums.

About a month later, I took a tour of the mine with some members of the Denver-based Energy Fuels team. Some mines were quiet, but Canyon Mine on the south side was bustling. Workers went about their business in fluorescent yellow protective gear and white hard hats, which I was mandated to wear for safety as well.

"The Native tribes are well within their rights to protest or oppose us in any way they see fit," a senior-level marketing executive told me. "Just as we're well within our rights to mine this deposit. We need electricity to run our cities, and that doesn't come from magical sources—it comes from mining, from oil and gas, from drilling and that sort of thing."

He explained that uranium mining is heavily regulated. "We're the safest, we're the healthiest, we do it the right way, we protect the environment. I just really don't think there's any chance we're going to have any impact to the Grand Canyon through our operations here."

As he spoke, I could tell he really believed what he was saying. Earlier that day, as we were eating lunch near the rim, he'd repeatedly told me how much he loved the Grand Canyon. But as I watched the massive machines clanking and whirring right behind him, hauling load after load of ore from thousands of feet below the surface, I had to wonder if there was any way an operation like this could be risk-free.

―

The team had agreed that Kevin and I were competent enough to tackle the next section of our thru-hike—a tricky, rarely traveled area—on our own. With their blessing, we set out into a section of the canyon known as the Godscape. The endless buttes, wind-sculpted ribs, and mazes of side drainages created a sense of overwhelming awe.

The cold and snow of winter had now melted into the lengthening days of March. To save weight, Kevin and I were carrying just a rain tarp and food. As long as we could find water, we could bend our bodies to sleep in nearly any flattish rocky depression atop our one-inch inflatable pads (which consistently punctured and deflated). It was amazing how comfortable a slab of granite or sandstone or a patch of gravel surrounded by cactus could feel after hiking for twelve hours.

One day, Rich Rudow sent us satellite text messages with coordinates to suspected potholes where we might find water. None of them worked out. Two of his most reliable potholes were filled with dust, forcing us to heighten our ability to read the landscape to survive. Our senses sharpened, and we began to pick up the subtlest hints pointing to water—signs we couldn't even put into words. Certain layers of rock held water longer than others. Side canyon depressions facing north with shady overhangs often protected small potholes. And sometimes there were subtle indications like more insects, more sheep droppings, or even ancient archeology markers like agave roasting pits that suggested water was near. Such roasting pits would typically be slightly cone-shaped, with clusters of agave plants and pottery shards often carpeting the area. Whenever we noticed them, springs or shadowed nooks with potholes of rainwater were often close by.

"Does that alcove look like it has potential?" Kevin would ask, and I'd nod silently, already scurrying ahead to investigate.

We were developing an almost primal intuition, the kind of awareness that must have kept people alive in this place for thousands of years. The canyon was teaching us to listen with more than our ears.

―

For safety reasons, Kevin and I chose to not hike during the height of summer, when temperatures could easily push well above 120 degrees. We waited for the monsoonal rains of late summer to replenish the hidden springs and oases that sustained life.

But even though our hiking mission was on hold, my cameras weren't. I wanted to document what tourist traffic in the canyon looked like when it went relatively unchecked.

Ever since my dory trip with Johno, I'd wondered what it would look and feel like to walk through Heli Alley—that miles-long stretch of canyon where helicopters swarmed like mosquitoes during every waking hour. I wanted to try to capture what all that air traffic looked like over time. So in mid-July, I recruited my friends Harlan Taney and Justin Clifton, both filmmakers and canyon lovers, to join me. We set off for Heli Alley to document how many helicopter flights traveled inside our most iconic national park in a day.

Cowering under a makeshift shade tarp, the three of us endured the furnace heat and did nothing but count and photograph helicopters. We clocked the temperature at 118 degrees at 4:00 p.m. By the end of the day, the drone and ringing of turbine engines reverberated in my ears. There's a reason Helicopter Alley has been described as a war zone—with a chopper landing approximately every five minutes, there's no time for your nervous system to recover from the sensory assault.

It occurred to me that there was a parallel here between the overallocated river and the airspace above it. Both were being loved to death. Although the so-called Hualapai exemption didn't name a limit on the number of flights per day, it was clear that this legislation had been written with a far smaller number of tourists in mind. We were operating beyond carrying capacity, both in the air and with the water. Yet now that we had allocated these resources, it would be extremely hard to claw them back.

When I got home, I loaded a day's worth of photographs into Photoshop and enlisted the help of a fellow photographer to create what is known as a photographic merge: a layering of images to show a cumulative effect over time. My merge showed a sky choked with 363 individual helicopter flights on two different flight paths during an eight-hour period, as well as a river filled bumper-to-bumper with the motorized pontoon boats that whisk helicopter passengers away on a short jaunt up the river.

A photographic merge illustrates the amount of daily air and river traffic through Heli Alley.

Afterward, I interviewed Hualapai tribal members about their views on their newest tourism success. I learned that before the helicopter landings were approved, more than a third of households on the reservation lived below the poverty line. They told me the operation brought in almost $50 million annually for the tribe—money that funded services like police, EMS, and college scholarships, as well as annual profit-sharing checks to tribal members. Still, most of the profits seemed to flow to the helicopter companies and the developers, and sometimes it felt like the tribe's money ran through its hands like water. As one tribe member lamented, "Where does that money go? We don't see it."

Other tribal members shrugged at the suggestion that rich tourists in helicopters were spoiling the peace and quiet for *other* rich tourists on foot and in boats. Most of the canyon was still permeated by deep silence, as Kevin and I well knew. The helicopter zone represented only about 4 percent of the whole. Why kick up a fuss about a few noisy miles of river when it was providing jobs and services to people who badly needed them? Why should the ideals and preferences of relatively privileged backcountry hikers and rafters take precedence over the needs of a people whose connection to this place went back centuries before this park was even conceived?

One of the people I spoke with was none other than Bennett Wakayuta—the Hualapai elder I'd encountered gathering wild tobacco when I took the dory trip with Johno. Since that first meeting on the river, I'd learned a little more about Bennett's story. In 2010, he'd been between jobs and newly sober when his girlfriend (now wife) said, "Grab your shorts, you're going on a river trip with the tribe's cultural monitoring department—and it leaves in thirty minutes."

That river trip was a turning point. "The elders told me, 'The river can either end your life or it can change your life,'" he said. "I already knew the river could end a life because my brother had drowned in it a couple years before. But I didn't know the river was going to change my life—reconnect me to my spirituality and turn me full Hualapai."

Now, sitting across from Bennett as the helicopters droned nearby, I told him I'd counted 363 individual flights that day (according to records, some days see more than 400). He shook his head in disgust. "We need to make money, but the helicopters are a mess," he said. "We are a hunting tribe. How can we hunt if we fill our lands with noise?"

The dilemma facing the Hualapai was the same one I'd seen up and down the river: communities trying to balance economic survival with protecting their natural and cultural heritage. Just as farmers had to choose between irrigated fields and a living river, and cities had to choose between building new subdivisions and keeping water flowing to existing ones, the tribes found themselves choosing between tourism dollars and cultural preservation. Everyone who depended on the Colorado River was caught in a seemingly impossible bind.

My helicopter merge photo was my attempt to help figure out a balance for all. The ordinary Tuesday I documented felt and sounded excessive. Later, I would take a helicopter tour myself to experience and document it from that perspective. I shared the ride with a friendly Australian family who loved seeing the canyon—but after getting their morning yogurt splattered all over their faces by another helicopter's rotor wash, they told me it seemed a bit overcrowded.

In October, Kevin and I rejoined Rich and Kelly for the last leg of our journey. They would help us carry food and give us endless, loving grief as we pushed through the final few miles. Walking through the westernmost edge of the canyon, I noted that the gems and majesty of this rocky cathedral were not limited to the more popular pockets that lay far to the east. Out here, we discovered more ancient art, more bighorn sheep, more potsherds, and more rattlesnakes, coyotes, mule deer, bobcats, quail, frogs, tarantulas, and tarantula hawks than we had in the previous six hundred miles of our journey.

As we moved up and down through the final reaches of the canyon, I couldn't help but think about the threads connecting this place to the stories I'd been documenting throughout the rest of the watershed. The same forces that had dried up the delta and shrunk Lake Powell were at work here too: development pressure, resource extraction, and the human desire to monetize even the wildest or most sacred of spaces.

To truly preserve the Grand Canyon, we would have to learn to let it exist in its own right—not merely as entertainment for easily distracted humans. We would have to listen to the people who have been protecting it for generations and recognize that its grandeur and beauty, often soaked in silence or shrouded in starlight, are irreplaceable.

~

On a Sunday afternoon in early November, thirteen months after we first entered the canyon, Kevin and I found ourselves staring at three rusty fence posts pounded into the dirt. The northwestern corner of Grand Canyon National Park was so remote that this was the only marker delineating its boundary.

Standing at those boundary posts, I thought about all the arbitrary lines humans had drawn across this watershed: states fighting over water rights, the border between the United States and Mexico, the invisible lines dividing tribal lands from national parks. The Colorado River recognized none of these borders. Not only that, but the threats it faced—from drought, climate change, pollution, and overdevelopment—affected the entire river, even if we set aside certain sections to "protect."

What struck me the most was how differently we were all responding to the crisis unfolding before our eyes. Politicians bickered over water allocations while reservoirs dropped to record lows. Developers built new subdivisions in the desert without any guarantee that there would be enough water to wash dishes in those shiny new kitchens. Over breakfasts at local diners, people talked about the drought like a temporary inconvenience rather than a foreshadowing of the new normal in the West.

Meanwhile, the river itself was indifferent to these human dramas—our greed and hubris, our wishful thinking and self-delusion, our Upper and Lower Basin politics. It was just following the laws of gravity, doing its best to flow downstream, carrying however much water we'd left in it—a subtle and profound sign that we should ask less.

I'd subconsciously been drawing my own arbitrary lines—telling myself I was just a photographer, just a witness passing through. But standing there at the very edge of the park, I realized the river had been washing away my carefully constructed neutrality mile by mile.

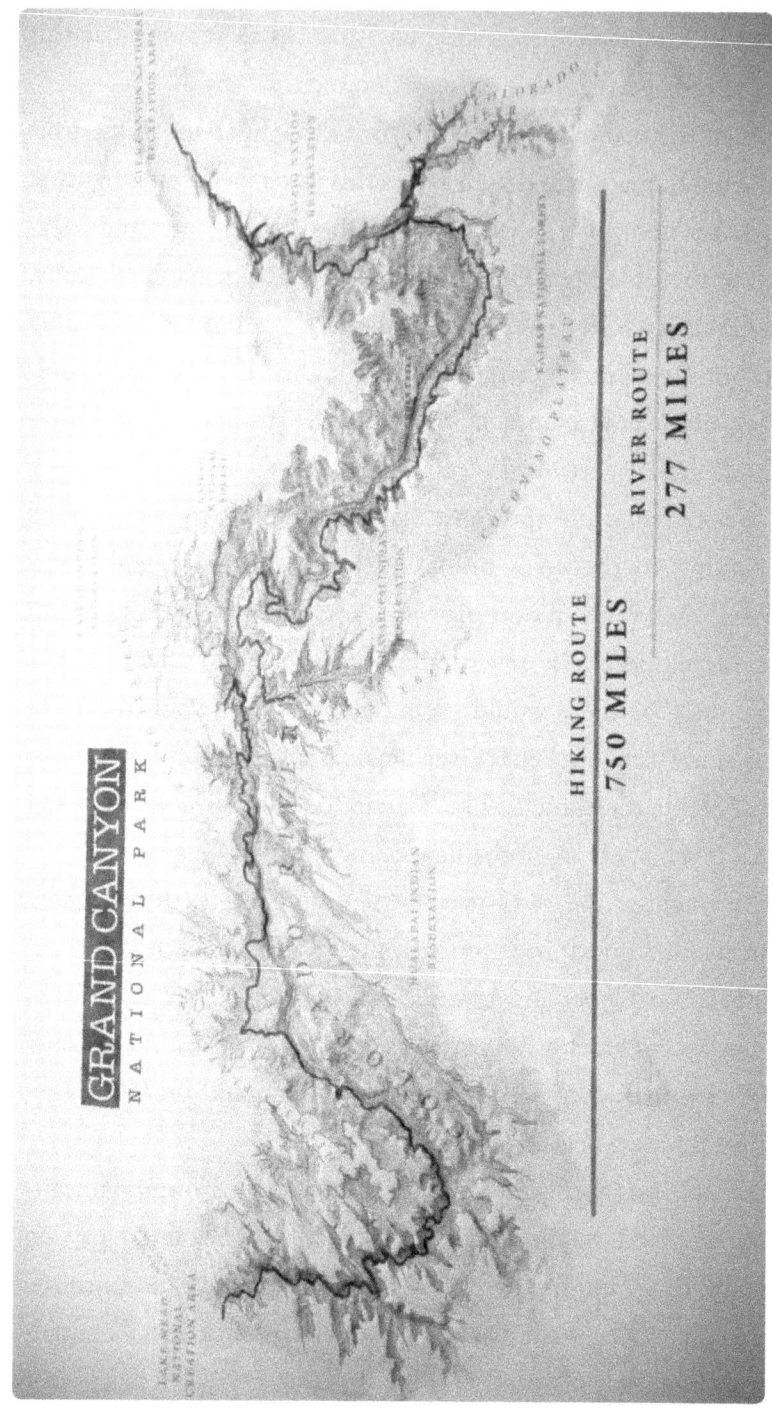

This map of the Grand Canyon illustrates the route that the author and Kevin Fedarko traveled during their hike.

As Kevin and I strode through the posts and exited Grand Canyon National Park, he turned to me.

"High five, man," he said, lifting a sunburned hand.

"High five."

We shared a celebratory howl and a round of sweaty hugs. Rich cried a few tears of amazement. "I can't believe you guys actually made it," he said.

Then, we kept hiking. As we scrambled into a setting sun with scraped arms and legs, we reflected on the lessons the canyon had taught us. Even though it appeared too vast and solid to be marred by human beings, the canyon had revealed a breathtaking fragility. After spending so many months drenched in the silence and magic of this natural wonder of the world, I knew there was only one place that looked and sounded like this. The question was whether we would fight to keep it that way.

Chapter 7

A Voice for Rivers

Kevin and I had barely been out of the canyon for twenty-four hours when a call came from *National Geographic*: "Congratulations, Pete. You and Kevin Fedarko have made our list for Adventurers of the Year."

I felt proud and a tiny bit dismayed. I didn't want the "adventure" aspect of the trip to overshadow the advocacy. For me, the important thing wasn't the fact that Kevin and I had gone on a really long, humbling, risky "walk in the park," but that the beauty and silence of the canyon were being threatened by pressures like tourism and mining.

Still, it felt incredibly validating to be recognized for the scope of our vision, our dogged persistence, and the work we'd put into amplifying the voices of the Native peoples we'd spoken with along the way. Being celebrated as a National Geographic Adventurer made the squeaking in my ankle ligaments, my newly erratic pulse, and the infected cactus needles still lodged in my shins feel that much more worthwhile.

The award meant we had been inducted into the ranks of people like mountaineer Pasang Lhamu Sherpa Akita, who had assisted in rescue efforts after the 2015 earthquake in Nepal, and wildlife biologist Steve Boyes, who completed a 1,578-mile expedition down the Cuito and Okavango rivers in southern Africa to document a 10,000-square-mile wetland he described as "the beating heart of our planet."

The Adventurer of the Year award opened doors Kevin and I couldn't have imagined. Suddenly we were getting invitations to speak at conferences and events all over the world.

We did a sixteen-city speaking tour with National Geographic Live, and I brought in the Grand Canyon Trust—the nonprofit that had worked behind the scenes with Renae Yellowhorse and Save the Confluence. Afterward, we signed with a speakers bureau to manage all of our contracts and travel.

"These speaking tours are more of a grind than I expected," Kevin said during one of the many similarly toned conversations we had during this time.

"I'm still getting used to sleeping in an actual bed instead of on a ground cloth," I said. "We should ask them to freeze-dry our meals, or just give us almonds and dried mangoes for lunch."

As much fun as it was to joke about all the speaking gigs we were doing now that our grueling hike was over, the truth is that this was fortuitous timing. Old-fashioned magazine assignments were getting harder and harder to come by as the world of print continued to be decimated by digital media. Technologies like Instagram made it easier than ever to access imagery and content related to anything your heart desired; you no longer had to wait for a glossy print issue of *National Geographic* to land in your mailbox to see astounding images of the world's most remote places.

Even though I would always be a photographer and filmmaker at heart, I knew that I was incredibly lucky to have a parallel career as a speaker fall into my lap. Kevin and I rehearsed our presentations ad nauseum, creating dramatic handoffs that amplified the comedic effect. We leaned into our characters: me the endlessly optimistic Tigger, and Kevin the doomsday Eeyore doling out dire warnings.

Audiences loved it when we made self-deprecating jokes about our lack of preparation—as if we were two bros who had set down our beers, laced up some hiking boots, and bumbled into the canyon—but we made sure to emphasize how the journey changed us and what we learned. We reminded our audiences how despite the support of friends and canyon lovers, our ongoing food cache preparations, permit work, and skill, the canyon repeatedly served us humble pie. That is the wonder of our parks. They are wild and remote, and they teach each generation lasting lessons about our connection to nature and ourselves—which requires respect. This kind of hike, even when it's filled with follies, shouldn't ever be done on a lark.

I also continued to do many talks on my own. Although I felt anything but neutral about the issues I was speaking about, I continued to let my photographs do the heavy lifting on the political side. Instead of saying, "We need to rethink dams and water rights" or "We need to restrict mining," I would simply say, "This is what I learned; this is what I saw." You don't have to be a tree-hugging environmentalist to look at a river run bone-dry and realize we have too many straws in the drink, or to see radioactive springs in the crown jewel of America's national park system and realize that mining poses a threat to people, animals, and the environment.

I learned that by letting my photos do the talking and not preaching at anyone, I could keep a line of communication open with people who might otherwise assume that conservation is only for the crunchy. I got invitations from ranching associations and hedge funds, people you wouldn't normally associate with a pro-environment message. It thrilled me to think that the stories I told might convince relatively powerful people to change their stances on water rights, agriculture, mining, and tourist development. These were the kind of people who could change the fate of an ecosystem with the stroke of a pen, or by making a big campaign contribution to one political candidate instead of another. If I could influence them to care about rivers, that was a powerful thing.

"You've been rubbing shoulders with some big wheels, Peto," my mom would say. "Don't let your britches get too big. Now help me cook dinner." As we prepped a salad, we chatted about my talks. "Your story is unique, but remember: People are generally good; they just sometimes don't know what to do. So help them—give them a feisty little nudge." She animated the word *nudge* with one of her signature dance flourishes, a jab of her arm and an infectious smile.

But as my public speaking career took off, it seemed that my body and mind were lagging further and further behind. I was still adapting to the noisy, overstimulating world above the rim. I missed the deep silence and simplicity of my time in the canyon—when everything I needed fit into a backpack, when all I had to do each day was cover some miles and find water along the way, and when I didn't need to create a persona or craft a narrative to keep an audience entertained.

I was still the same, simple, dirtbag Pete—the guy who loves skiing, jamming on mandolin, and telling stories around a campfire—yet my increasingly public life meant I had to create an avatar, a public-facing, slightly more buttoned-up self who looked and sounded like me, but wasn't exactly me. This was the opposite of the stripping-away I'd experienced in the canyon. In the canyon, I was breath, muscle, salt, and thirst. Entire days would pass when I would barely say a word. Now, my livelihood depended on me talking all the time.

"Do you ever miss the canyon?" I asked Kevin.

"Every day," he said.

"I feel like my vibe sensor got so attuned while we were down there. I could pick up on the slightest sound or motion or shift in the weather. And up here there's so much noise, I can barely feel those things."

The quiet in the canyon had been so remarkably deep that the microphones on my cameras often didn't work well. They would create buzzing sounds, and I later learned this happened because they'd never been calibrated to a such a high level of silence. Now, the "vibe sensor" I'd developed in that cauldron of silence made me extra sensitive to the drone of civilization. My home in Basalt, Colorado, population four thousand, wasn't exactly Manhattan, but I noticed cars, snowblowers, and amplified music in ways I hadn't before. When people hiked or skied past me with portable speakers, I'd ask them to turn their music off, feeling like an old curmudgeon. Couldn't they tell they were jamming the signal, making it harder to hear the subtle messages that nature was giving us all the time?

The hotels Kevin and I stayed in for speaking engagements felt overly sanitized and unnatural, and I yearned to bed down where I could see the stars instead of contending with yet another measured room with weird buzzes, city reflections, and crisp white sheets. I'd become so sensitive to light that I'd spend half an hour hunting down every last LED, draping shirts and towels over alarm clocks and thermostats, before I could finally fall asleep.

I often got lost finding my hotel room, mixing up the floor and room number with whichever one I'd stayed in the night before. Even though the canyon was vast, I'd always known exactly where I was—so why did I feel so disoriented here?

Back in April, the Canyon Mine shaft had hit groundwater and flooded. Ever since then, the mine had been pumping contaminated water out of the shaft and spraying it into the air in an effort to evaporate it. Meanwhile, birds and other animals continued to drink from the large ponds in which the contaminated water was being held, and toxic mist drifted across the landscape. It was horrifying to think that Carletta's predictions might be coming true, and that some of this contaminated water might be actively making its way to Supai.

For me, the Canyon Mine disaster added a new sense of urgency to finish my documentary film, *Into the Canyon*. People needed to know that this was happening just ten miles from Grand Canyon National Park. Yes, we need uranium for various purposes—but not as much as we need clean, drinkable water. When I thought back to how confidently the Energy Fuels representative had been when he told me the mine posed no threat, I was reminded of how much hubris human beings can show when there's a profit to be made.

On October 31, 2017—almost exactly one year after Kevin and I finished our hike—something else happened that made me remember why all this difficult work was worth it. The Navajo Nation held a special council meeting with the directive to vote on the Grand Canyon Escalade project, and I traveled to Window Rock, Arizona, with Kevin to film it.

Throughout the meeting—which spanned eight hours with few breaks—the council chambers were packed. Renae and her friends, wearing Save the Confluence T-shirts and traditional turquoise jewelry, occupied several rows of seats. Supporters of the Grand Canyon Escalade project sat with their arms folded, ready for a standoff. Over the years, Renae and her friends had gathered a whopping eighty-seven thousand signatures opposing the tramway, mostly by tabling at farmers markets and other community events, educating people about the true scale and impacts of the tram.

When it was the developer's turn to speak, he reminded the audience that the Navajo Nation would receive sales tax and hotel taxes from all the proposed attractions. Then he showed the audience a colorful bar chart.

"As the visitor count increases, the percentage of gross revenue that goes to the Navajo Nation increases, too," he said.

The numbers on the chart caught my eye. It showed that the Navajo Nation's cut would start at 8 percent, but when the Escalade project hit two million visitors, this number would rise to 18 percent.

I tried to imagine two million people walking around the confluence annually—not to mention eating, drinking, generating litter, and going to the bathroom. The thought made me sick. I could only imagine how Renae and her cohort felt.

After the developer finished his presentation, community members who opposed the tram got up one by one to ask questions and deliver testimony. They were gracious and eloquent, but steadfast in their opposition.

"What happens when the hotels say, 'Oh, by the way, we don't want to pay taxes?'" asked one person.

"I'm wondering about your comment saying this is about job creation," said another, "when actually it's the Navajo Nation that would be fronting the whole bill. You're not being honest, sir."

One elder stood up in the back of the room and spoke with passion. "You have not consulted with the water people. You have not consulted with the wind people."

As he spoke, people in the council chamber began to cheer and clap. I felt myself tearing up.

Finally, it was time for the council to vote. Everyone in the room seemed to writhe in anguish while the votes slowly came in one by one. I saw Renae hold her head in her hands, as if bracing herself for whatever was about to come. Across the room, the developers looked no less nervous than she did.

The television screen displaying each council member's vote began to fill up with red X's for "no," with only two green checkmarks for "yes." The council had sided with Save the Confluence in a landslide victory of 16–2. The meeting room erupted in joyous cheers and whoops. Renae burst into tears, and women crowded around to embrace her.

Outside the council chambers, I made my way over to Renae, my head spinning with surprise and disbelief. When I asked for a quick interview, she got straight to the point.

"No. More. Escalade," she said.

"They listened to us," her friend and colleague Rita Bilagody chimed in. "I'm going to go home and sleep for two days."

I understood the feeling. After months on the road and endless speaking engagements, my own heart and soul were sending signals that were getting harder and harder to ignore.

My body had been reshaped by the canyon, all excesses shaved away after months of subsisting on fewer calories than I was burning. I had gotten out of the habit of eating large meals, and gotten used to grazing on handfuls of nuts and seeds throughout the day. I had new aches and pains in my joints that were seemingly here to stay, and my face had weathered from the extreme sun exposure, aging me and giving me that leathery desert rat look.

The most concerning change was that my heart seemed to have developed an extra beat. I'd get a flutter and sometimes a long delay in my pulse, and feel the urge to lie down and sleep for a few minutes.

Back in Colorado, my heart fluctuations only seemed to be getting worse. Something was wrong, and I was beginning to realize that it might not just go away on its own. I also seemed to have extra cortisol running through my system. The friendly demeanor and wealth of patience I'd developed as a photographer was eroding; instead, I'd lose my cool and get frustrated with people easily. I wasn't sure if that was related to the heart flutter, or if it was due to the stress of the constant travel and speaking, but it pained me to see myself snapping at people like that. Airports and planes were making me edgy too, and I used to love traveling and flying. What was happening to me?

Finally, I dragged myself to a doctor who diagnosed me with atrial fibrillation (A-fib)—a condition where the upper chambers of the heart beat unpredictably and out of sync with the lower chambers.

"This is a direct result of physical stress and most likely hyponatremia," the doctor said. "The extreme dehydration and lack of sodium you experienced in the canyon literally rewired your heart."

He explained that even though I felt pretty good most of the time, my risk of stroke was massively increased, not to mention congestive heart failure and organ damage.

"You don't want to let this ride, Pete," he said. "This isn't the kind of thing you can walk off."

In December 2017, just a few days before Christmas, I traveled to Denver to undergo a nine-hour ablation procedure to correct the arrhythmia. Just twelve hours before the surgery was scheduled, I lost my cool on a call with a health insurance representative, who told me my procedure still wasn't approved but "should be." It felt like my sunny demeanor had been swallowed up by a storm cloud of anger and frustration. Although it was hard to explain to my family and friends, I was even more worried about losing my personality than I was about the flutter in my heart. My Tigger-like persona was turning more into Oscar the Grouch. I hoped the surgery would bring back the real me.

After the surgery, I stayed with my longtime friend Duke Beardsley while I recovered. For the first three days I was basically asleep, with his family's dog curled up next to me in bed. My first "outing" was a walk around his neighborhood, but I couldn't make it to the end of the driveway before returning to bed. Two weeks later, I felt much better than I had in a long time. My heart seemed to be working normally and my energy came back. I'd been like a frog in hot water, getting used to a declining baseline of health, forgetting what "good" really felt like. It's the same thing we do with our rivers, our snowpack, our climate: although we might notice a difference at first, we swiftly adapt, until the diminished health of our waterways starts to feel like "just the way things are."

One day, my speaking agent sent me my touring schedule for the next six months. Looking at it made me nauseous. In late January, I'd be giving a talk at the Outdoor Retailer conference, a massive event attended by thousands of people. Then, I'd immediately go on tour with National Geographic Live, speaking at performing arts centers in Portland, Seattle, Phoenix, Los Angeles, Chicago, Santa Barbara, and Kansas City, often for several nights in a row.

After every talk, there was often wining and dining, handshaking and photographs, then finally the return to a lonely hotel room where I would lie awake, jet-lagged and overstimulated. Talking to friends or family on the phone helped a little, but mostly it just made me miss them even more. Also, I hated being unable to stop complaining when I knew I had it so good.

"If everyone's smiling and clapping, why do I still feel like I'm speaking into a void?" I lamented to my mom on a visit to my parents' house between speaking engagements.

"I don't know, Peto," she said. "You have a voice, but you're not sure if that voice has influence. And honestly, you might never be able to measure your impact, or lack of impact, in a satisfying way. Come on, stop fretting and let's go play Ping-Pong."

She was patient and sympathetic, but I still wished I could drum up more genuine excitement or tell her funny stories instead of pouring out my angst. Ping-Pong helped sweeten our mood, although, as usual, she beat me. Considering the fact that she was nearly eighty, this both inspired me and stirred up a little vexation that I still couldn't beat her. As she celebrated her victory, she said, "Don't worry about it, Peto. Do what you can. That's all we can do."

Later that evening, my mind started reeling again. How could audiences in comfortable auditoriums ever know what it meant to be so thirsty that you start thinking about drinking your own urine? Did they understand that the photos I showed them documented not only the present, but glimpses of a parched and thirsty future that was coming for their own local waterways if we didn't change our approach to managing fresh water? Would they change their own behavior to help a river, or would they go on assuming that the dire message my photographs conveyed did not apply to them or their communities?

I had become a witness to water—but was anyone listening?

Chapter 8

The Wrong Kind of Quiet

"Kids, Moutie and I have something we want to tell you," said my dad.

"So you'd better listen up," my mom quipped.

Johno, Kate, and I were all gathered around the kitchen table at the ranch, late afternoon sun streaming through the big windows onto the worn wooden table where we'd eaten thousands of meals together. Outside, I could hear red-winged blackbirds trilling in a cottonwood outside.

"We've decided to donate a conservation easement to the Aspen Valley Land Trust," Mom said. "The whole ranch—all of it—will be protected in perpetuity."

"Well, *I* wanted to build a shopping mall on it, but your mom overruled me," Dad cut in.

My mom rolled her eyes. "Oh, good grief."

"A fast-food joint would be a good addition to the pasture," he said, gesturing out the window. "And think of how convenient it would be!"

As they began to lightheartedly tease each other, I felt something catch in my throat. It wasn't just that I was proud of my parents for placing their environmental values at the center of their lives. It was the way they still made their own comedy duo after being together for decades. Although I yearned for deep companionship, I'd always put my career first, and in moments like these I felt the weight of that sacrifice.

I was staying busy working on my film, *Into the Canyon*, and writing the companion text for my photography book *The Grand Canyon: Between River and Rim*, but somehow that all felt insignificant compared to what my parents had achieved: a stable marriage, a happy family, and an enduring legacy in the community.

As the conversation shifted to elephant conservation in Kenya—another one of my parents' favorite topics—I tried to remind myself that my relationship woes weren't that big a deal in the grand scheme of things. There were wild animals facing extinction, rivers being sucked dry, and communities with serious housing shortages or being poisoned by heavy industry and resource extraction. No one gets all they want in life, nor should we. Life is adversity and how you get up from it when it beats you down.

On the drive home to Basalt, I tuned in to the local news station:

> For the first time in the Colorado River's modern history, all seven states have agreed to mandatory water cuts. Arizona and Nevada will take the biggest hits, losing 18 percent and 7 percent of their allocations, respectively. California, the river's biggest user, will contribute through conservation programs. Meanwhile, the Upper Basin states will implement so-called "demand management programs" in which farmers, cities, and other

water users will be paid to reduce their water use without losing their legally allocated water rights.

Suddenly, the sorrow that had settled over me at the ranch lifted. In a flash, I remembered that all the river advocates I'd filmed over the years really were making a difference. Their efforts had paved the way for this agreement to happen, incomplete and imperfect as it was. And if I could support that effort with my camera, I wasn't wasting my time.

≈

Signed into law on April 16, 2019, the Colorado River Drought Contingency Plan wasn't perfect—it was more like a tourniquet than the long and complicated surgery the Colorado River Compact required—but it was something.

As the agreements kicked in, Las Vegas passed a law that prohibited water-guzzling grass in medians, along roads, and in business parks; restricted evaporative cooling systems; and banned golf courses from using Colorado River water to keep their fairways green. Arizona announced that it would stop approving any new housing developments on the edges of Phoenix whose plans depended on groundwater. In my home state of Colorado, a water conservation group worked to reimburse ranchers who voluntarily fallowed their fields, or switched to less water-intensive crops to reimburse their losses.

Now, when I gave talks, I had something to point to. "California, Utah, Nevada, Arizona, Colorado, New Mexico, and Wyoming are now working together to reduce how much water they're sucking out of the Colorado," I could say. "And that's a really big deal."

For the first time in years—ever since the pulse flow in March of 2014—it felt like I wasn't simply the bearer of bad news. I had evidence that collective action was possible, even in the context of a long history of bitter struggle over a limited resource.

"Don't get me wrong; the Drought Contingency Plan is a Band-Aid on top of a Band-Aid," I'd say in my talks, echoing what my friend Taylor Hawes with the Nature Conservancy once told me. "It's a reactionary, short-term fix, and we need to do better. But what it *does* do is prove that we can get by on less water, if we make up our minds to do so."

I was flying high, feeling a renewed sense of energy, purpose, and what I like to call "earned hope."

Then in March 2020, the COVID-19 pandemic arrived.

Overnight, the speaking engagements that had both energized and drained me over the past four years vanished into thin air. Nobody was willing to pack into a crowded auditorium with a deadly virus in the air—and in many instances, they were forbidden from doing so out of caution for public health. With plane travel newly risky, magazines weren't handing out assignments, either. Several international projects I had lined up were abruptly canceled. The prospect of facing months of lockdown alone filled me with dread.

I self-quarantined at my home in Basalt, video-chatting with friends and family on my laptop. My home, which had once felt like a cozy place to rest and recover between adventures, quickly started to feel like a cage. Thanks in part to my career, I've never embraced my domestic side beyond making a home-cooked meal or optimistically planting a garden, which would inevitably die after I took off on an assignment just when it needed me most.

As many mixed feelings as I had about my exhausting speaking schedule, its sudden disappearance left a void I didn't know how to fill.

"Our careers are over," I said to Kevin over the course of one of many despairing phone calls. "It was already hard enough to get assignment work before the pandemic. Now, people like us are dead in the water."

It felt like the rug was being pulled out from under me just when I was reaping the rewards of everything I'd worked so hard for. All those years of thin assignment budgets, fizzling relationships, cheese going green in the fridge while I camped in remote, dangerous, and uncomfortable places, the injuries, the stomach viruses, the heart surgery—I hadn't done all that so I could end up unemployed and hopeless.

"This feels just like the place where I saw the Colorado River shrivel up and die," I told Kevin. "Like my life was supposed to keep going, keep flowing to the ocean, and instead it just screeched to a halt in the middle of nowhere."

The silence I'd celebrated in the Grand Canyon—filled with the whisper of bat wings and the bleating of distant sheep—was replaced by a dead, anxious void.

For the first time in over a decade, I wasn't chasing water. I wasn't documenting decline or cheering on restoration. I wasn't giving talks or filming protests or meeting new people whose lives revolved around the river. Instead, I spent my afternoons doomscrolling COVID-19 news and worrying. Friends and neighbors were getting sick, and some of them were dying. The doctor who'd given me my A-fib diagnosis after I came out of the Grand Canyon was one of them. Each new piece of bad news deepened my sense of gloom.

I started drinking more than usual—an extra beer or glass of wine in the evening, just enough to take the edge off my boredom and restlessness. It wasn't a dramatic flameout; it was more like I was slowly deflating. Each day seemed to melt into the next, with little to mark the passage of time. I kept yearning for something to *happen*—but what?

My film *Into the Canyon* had been nominated for an Emmy, but lockdown meant there would be no in-person awards ceremony. Instead, when the awards show aired in September, I hosted a black-tie barbecue in my backyard, live streaming the event on a projector while my family and a handful of friends snacked on pulled pork and cornbread. My nephew Jasper wore my grandfather's top hat. The Emmy ended up going to a very deserving film called *The Serengeti Rules*, which was directed by my friend Nick Brown, who was watching the ceremony on Zoom from London, 2:00 a.m. his time, by himself. We all toasted him from Colorado, raising our glasses to the camera.

In December, I caught COVID-19 and had Christmas alone, sick as a dog and deeply depressed. From where I was standing, I couldn't imagine that I'd ever get back the kind of adventure, camaraderie, and, most important, sense of purpose I'd felt before.

When I went to visit my parents after I was no longer contagious, I offered to show them the photos I'd taken from the night of the Emmys.

"The what?" said my dad.

"The barbecue we had for the Emmys," I said. "Remember? It was a couple months ago. We all dressed in tuxedos, Jasper wore your father's top hat, and we sat around the backyard watching the ceremony on a projector." My stomach dropped. "You remember, right?"

There was a long pause. "Oh yeah, sure," said my dad. "Of course I remember. That was a good time."

Something about the way he said that didn't seem right. It felt like he was covering for something, the way we all sometimes pretend to remember things we've actually forgotten: a person's name, a commitment we've made, an article we skimmed instead of deeply reading.

Later, I took my mom aside in the kitchen.

"Is it just me, or does it seem like Dad's forgetting a lot of things?" I said.

She nodded. "He has an appointment with a specialist next month," she said. "They're going to test him for early Alzheimer's. For the most part, he's his same old self, but some days it feels like his short-term memory is on hiatus."

Over the next few months, I began to notice the way that simple conversations with my dad would loop back on themselves. He'd tell the same story a few times, or ask me the same question over and over. I would get frustrated, then feel ashamed of myself for my frustration. It took a lot of effort to remain cheerful and patient, to not let my annoyance show. After all, it wasn't his fault he couldn't remember.

"Pabo wants to act like nothing's different," I said to my mom.

"Well, that's because he's in denial," she said. "And also, he's probably terrified."

That gave me pause. Would I act any differently if the familiar mental pathways I'd taken my whole life began drying up one by one? If the things that made me "me" started fading, and my memories began to blow away like autumn leaves from a tree?

My whole life, both of my parents had been so strong and vibrant. They weren't the type of people who lost their sparkle in midlife; if anything, they'd grown funnier and more exuberant the older they got. My mom still loved playing Tin Pan Alley songs and Chopin études on the piano, and my dad loved to ramble around the ranch with the dogs, seeing which birds were visiting from their migration route. Sandhill cranes were his favorite. He could mimic their calls closely. I am sure I saw him conversing with a pair once as they soared overhead and then descended for a closer look. For years, I'd been documenting the decline of a river; now, I realized, I was getting to the age where my parents' decline would be the next big heartbreak.

One day, I tried to get my parents to open up about their deaths. "Mom, Dad, do you want to be cremated or buried? Where do you want to be . . . sprinkled?"

My mom laughed, and my dad looked a little insulted.

"I don't want to be sprinkled," he said. "I want you to throw me out of the plane from the back seat in total, in full, over rocks."

"Oh Jesus," groaned my mom.

My dad's serious expression cracked into a grin, and I realized he was pulling our legs. "Pabo," I said, "I'm asking a real question. Do you guys want to be sprinkled together or far apart?"

"Depends how the day goes," he quipped, and both my parents' shoulders shook with laughter at a private joke you could probably only understand after sixty years of marriage.

"What about you, Mom? Do you want to be sprinkled someplace?"

She shook her head. "No," she said, glancing down with uncharacteristic shyness. "I have a burial site in what used to be an old lake basin, and you can't see anybody. It's kinda special."

I felt my throat well up with tears. I hadn't realized that my mom had such a specific plan for her own death—that she was thinking about her mortality, even if my dad preferred to brush such conversations off. The place she'd chosen—a dried-up lake bed, now surrounded with sagebrush—sounded both sublime and peaceful. It made me think of all the dried-up places I'd photographed along the Colorado: hidden nooks that had once hummed, buzzed, and whirred with life, and were now quiet and forgotten.

Driving back to Basalt that evening, I kept thinking about my dad's memory lapses and my mom's attempt to stay cheerful despite the mounting losses. Maybe it was a good thing this pandemic had forced me to stay home for a while and spend more time with them. I could spend the rest of my life documenting the Colorado, but I would only have my parents around for a few more years, another decade at the most. Human lives are so short compared to rivers, but the people we lose keep on shaping us long after they're gone.

The pandemic winter stretched on, each day blending into the next. I tried to keep myself busy with editing tasks, or researching treatments for Alzheimer's, but some days it seemed easier to let the depression win—to stop fighting the current and let myself drift into a state of living hibernation.

I was sliding into a dark place. I needed something to give me hope. Then in the spring of 2021, I got a call from an old friend. "Pedro!" he said. "How'd you feel about shaking off those pandemic blues and coming on a backcountry ski trip in Idaho?"

For the first time in months, I felt my heart lift.

"For real or are you messing with me?" I said.

"For real."

"Count me in!"

Chapter 9

Shifting Course

The place my friend had found was a remote summer cabin, which was snowmobile access–only in winter. Everyone who came from a mix of friend groups was required to pass a COVID-19 test beforehand. When I got to the log cabin, I opened a heavy wooden door and the first person I met was Heidi McCabe Bitter. She had come with the side of the friend group I knew less well. I was struck by her eyes—the most vivid blue I'd ever seen, like high-altitude lakes in the summer.

As we chatted, I immediately felt a sense of familiarity around her that made me forget I was meeting her for the first time. She had what my mom would call a high EQ—an ability to read the room and make everyone feel at ease.

"So what do you do when you're not riding snowmobiles to secret lodges?" I asked.

"I'm an executive assistant at a financial firm in New York City," she said. "But honestly, I'm trying not to think about work too much this week." She gestured at the snow-covered mountains. "This is my first time in Idaho and I'm blown away."

Heidi was still learning to ski, but she was athletic and graceful, and determined to improve. I was smitten. By the end of the week, we were an item. On our last night at the cabin, Heidi turned to me with a sly expression.

"This is terrible," she said, "but I think I got exposed to COVID somehow. I don't think it's a good idea for me to fly back to New York tomorrow."

"Oh no," I said. "You'd be a danger to the other travelers. You'd better come back to Basalt with me while you recover. I'm guessing I've been exposed as well." The reality was Heidi would be heading back east to work remotely, anyway. Why not do it where I lived instead?

Although we joked among ourselves about COVID exposure, neither of us took the virus lightly. We both had friends and family with high-risk immune systems, and we both knew others who had died. Perhaps that inspired a bit of a carpe-diem attitude in both of us. If we didn't spend time together now, who knew when we'd get another chance?

The next couple of months were a whirlwind of emotions and logistics. Heidi extended her stay in Colorado, working remotely from my house in Basalt while we figured out what we were doing. The place that had felt like a prison during the darkest days of the pandemic felt cozy and alive with her there. We went skiing and skating on alpine lakes; we took long walks, and cooked elaborate meals in my tiny kitchen while listening to *ranchera* music. She called my house the Bear Den, and then started calling me Bear.

I was falling in love fast, but the excitement I felt was tempered by fear. Post-lockdown, Heidi's job had been relocated to Florida.

Every few weeks, she had to fly back east for work, and I'd be reminded of how temporary all of this was. How could we make our relationship work when it was stretched across two thousand miles? How would we solve the puzzle of work and geography? What were we *doing*?

"I love it here," Heidi said one evening when we were sitting on my porch in Basalt. "But I can't live like this forever. We're always in different time zones, always out of sync with each other. There's just not enough time together to build a shared life. And once the pandemic restrictions ease up, you'll be traveling all the time for assignments or to give talks and it will only get harder."

We agreed to take a break, but three months later, we were planning a trip together.

"I don't know how to make this work," I told her. "All I know is I want you in my life. And I am *not* going to let my job get in the way."

I kept thinking about my parents, who'd been married for sixty years and still made each other laugh every day, even and perhaps especially as my dad's memory began to slip away. I wanted to build something like that with Heidi, no matter what challenges we had to overcome to get there.

But just because I refused to let work get in the way of my relationship with Heidi didn't mean I wasn't still craving a film project. By midsummer, with Heidi back east for a work stint and my own calendar still disturbingly empty, I found myself scrolling through my contacts, looking for anyone who might throw me a lifeline. That's how I ended up calling up my friend Matt Rice, the director of the Colorado branch of the nonprofit American Rivers.

"Matt," I said, after we did our usual catching up, "I'm losing my mind here. The film and photography industry has completely tanked since the pandemic, and I'm sitting around my house with literally nothing to do."

I told him about the sudden quiet that had fallen over my life. I'd done a few talks via Zoom, but it was hard to connect or feel value in the remote monologues. My empty calendar gave me time to get outside, often alone in the mountains, but I worried incessantly about my parents and family and was always looking for ways to help. I knew I had it better than many people, but as sheepish as I felt about my relative comfort, that didn't stop me from complaining about the sense of purpose I'd lost.

"At least you guys can still work remotely," I went on. "I'm used to being on location, working with crews, having structure. Now I feel like I'm shipwrecked on some desert island. Heidi's back east, and I've replaced some of my purpose with vino."

Matt laughed, then caught me up on his own work. "American Rivers is taking another shot at getting Wild and Scenic designation for the Gila River right now," he said.

"Do you think it's going to pass?"

"It'll pass if I have anything to say about it," Matt said. "Even with all the dams and diversions, it's still the last free-flowing river in New Mexico. From the headwaters in the Gila Wilderness, it flows free for 250 miles before hitting the Coolidge Dam. That's extremely rare these days." He paused. "Then again, people in New Mexico have been fighting for Wild and Scenic designation for this stretch of the Gila for years to no avail. This is just the latest attempt. I'm hopeful, but I'm not holding my breath."

The Gila River originates in western New Mexico and flows west, joining the Colorado River near Yuma, Arizona.

"What would Wild and Scenic do for the Gila?" I asked.

"A lot of things. No new dams, no clear-cutting, no new mining claims or mineral leases, stricter regulations on the ones that are already there. . . . " He trailed off. "It's not a silver bullet, but it would make a massive difference to the wilderness we have left."

"Did I read somewhere that riverboats used to travel down the Gila?" I asked.

"All the way to Phoenix," Matt said. "That was before all the agriculture. Now, it just barely reaches the Colorado, and only in big water years. Most of the time it runs dry just south of the Ashurst-Hayden Dam."

We both fell silent for a moment. Matt was one of the few people I knew who truly understood the grief of watching a river run dry.

"Well, I'll be rooting for you, buddy," I said. "I know your work can be a slog sometimes, but you're fighting the good fight."

"You know, Pete," said Matt, "American Rivers just decided to fund a documentary about the Gila to build support for the Wild and Scenic legislation. And you'd be the perfect guy to make it. Let me connect you with Mike Fiebig, the guy who runs our Southwest program. He and his wife paddled the entire Green and Colorado rivers from source to sea. You'll have a lot to talk about."

~

The invitation from Matt put a much-needed spring back in my step. I called up Mike and told him how excited I was about a Gila trip.

"We have to go soon," he said. "It's already the tail end of the water year on the Gila, and we'll be lucky to squeeze in a four-day trip before water levels are too low for even packrafts to navigate."

As soon as we nailed down the details, I called up Heidi.

"I got an assignment!" I said. "It's on the Gila River, in New Mexico."

Heidi laughed. "You sound like a puppy who's finally been thrown a ball," she said. "Matt must have really taken pity on you."

I spent the next few weeks doing what I loved best: planning an adventure. I organized my camera kit, studied maps of the river, and read up on its history. I drove my truck down to Durango, where Mike lived, and he and I caravanned to the put in—a solid ten-hour drive.

Before I knew it, I was standing on the banks of the Gila River with Mike, about to push our packrafts into what was admittedly a rather tepid and unimpressive flow. I looked at the warm trickle, then raised my eyebrows at Mike.

"Is this going to be enough water to paddle in?"

He shrugged apologetically. "The river's been running lower and drying up sooner," he said. "It's sad to see. You probably already know this, but many scientists are saying that climate change is going to cause permanent aridification in the Southwest. The whole state is going to turn into a desert, and the lusher, wetter areas like this one are going to be gone for good if we don't protect them. It's so much like the main Colorado—this tributary is facing the exact same pressures, but it's worse because we're further south."

He shoved his packraft into the water.

"Don't get me wrong," he said as he climbed in. "Ecological memory is amazing, but it's not indestructible. The way we're changing the climate, a lot of these plants and animals simply *can't* come back. We can conserve all the land we want, but what good is it if it's all burned to a crisp?"

I thought back to the pulse flow I'd witnessed in 2014. At the time, I'd been impressed by the way that crustaceans, birds, beavers, and fish reappeared as if by magic when we added back just a tiny amount of water. Although on some level I knew it was wishful thinking, there was a part of me that wanted to believe that ecosystems would spring back to life if we only gave them half a chance. We had hit the *pause* button on nature with all our industry and engineering, but we could hit the *play* button anytime, and the vanished habitats would reappear.

Mike's words reminded me of the complexity of the situation. Yes, some amount of restoration is possible—but there are also tipping points beyond which certain ecosystems are gone for good. Aridification was already happening in New Mexico, with an average temperature increase of 5 to 7 degrees Fahrenheit predicted over the next fifty years. Along with hotter temperatures, New Mexico was seeing thinner snowpacks, more frequent wildfires, and a major decline in river flow. The plants and animals that had thrived in a cooler, wetter Southwest were disappearing, and the habitats that sustained them would simply not be able to exist in a hotter, drier climate, no matter what kinds of protections we placed on the land.

I joined Mike in the water, and we started to paddle. It was hard to keep the reality of aridification in my mind as we glided through the headwaters. Life teemed around us—dragonflies, tadpoles, amphibians—all signs of healthy water quality. I was equally struck by the rich archaeological history embedded in the surrounding landscape.

"The Gila River headwaters have been inhabited for at least six thousand years," Mike explained. "In fact, the Native peoples here built over five hundred miles of canals to irrigate their crops."

Mountains and hills stretched upward from the banks in all directions. It was harsh too: hot, prickly, but also wooded. This tough desert forest felt like another world. This explained the long, meandering, curvy road that took hours to reach the put in.

I tried to imagine people building five hundred miles of irrigation canals before modern machinery, and my mind boggled. People have always used diverted water for their own ends—the difference is, we never did it at such a colossal scale that we made entire rivers run dry until recent decades. Our technologies have advanced much faster than our environmental protection laws, and rivers like the Gila are paying the price.

―

That afternoon, Mike and I paddled by a group of locals relaxing by the river in folding camp chairs—women ranging in age from around thirty to seventy-five, decked out in sunglasses and sandals. We chatted about the pandemic and how it had made nature access more important than ever. I asked them what the Gila meant to them. One of the women answered, "This is our getaway. This is our therapy. This is our everything. It's vital to who we are as a family and as a community." The others quickly agreed, telling me they wouldn't be who they were without the river.

I remembered the people in Mexico who had seen their beloved Colorado reduced to dust. They didn't only lose water: they lost play, celebration, identity, and, yes, therapy. What would happen to these women if the Gila met a similar fate?

The women's body language communicated a deep familiarity —a sense of being at home. These weren't wide-eyed tourists bumbling in for an afternoon of fun in the sun, but locals in the deepest sense of the word—people whose very sense of self was shaped by the river's presence.

I recognized that body language. I'd seen it expressed by countless people when I visited them in their backyard rivers: the Mexicans celebrating on the banks of the Colorado during the pulse flow, the Indians praying on the banks of the Ganges, and the river guides paddling Lava Falls in the Grand Canyon. When you know and love a place deeply, it shows in the relaxed set of your shoulders and the sparkle in your eyes. We are animated by the places we love—they literally give us life. What happens to that life when those places dry up?

~

As Mike and I floated on, I reflected on Aldo Leopold, the forest service employee who grew to love this place so much that he worked to protect it as wilderness at a time when few people outside of New Mexico had even heard of the Gila mountains, and when many people thought of wilderness only as something to be conquered and tamed. In explaining the value of wilderness, he wrote:

> Are these things worth preserving? This is the vital question. I cannot give an unbiased answer. I can only picture the day that is almost upon us when canoe travel will consist [of] paddling in the noisy wake of a motor launch and portaging through the back yard of a summer cottage. When that day comes, canoe travel will be dead, and dead, too, will be a part of our Americanism. (Aldo Leopold, "Wilderness as a Form of Land Use," *Journal of Land and Public Utility Economics*, October 1925)

However, even though the wilderness designation Leopold achieved for the Gila Wilderness Area prevented the construction of major roads and tourist infrastructure, it didn't contain protections for the actual *water* in the Gila River. That's why the push for Wild and Scenic designation was so important.

A little way down the river, we were joined by Simon Sotelo, a community organizer with a nonprofit called New Mexico Wild. When I asked him about the history of trying to get a Wild and Scenic designation for the Gila, he sighed.

"The first time around, the local community wasn't really consulted, much less put in charge of the effort. This time, we're asking the community directly: How would Wild and Scenic protection for the Gila help you? Why do you want to protect your river?"

I thought of the women we'd met lounging by the river, who described the place in terms of their mental health and relationships—things that couldn't be measured in cubic feet per second or economic impact studies.

"So you're saying conservation has to start with the people who are local with a capital L," I said.

"Exactly," Simon said. "Ask the local people what *they* feel they should be doing—not what outsiders think they should be doing. Then they can make an educated decision about whether or not a certain project is something they want to get behind."

That made a lot of sense—it seemed obvious. But getting locals organized and together in some of these instances was a challenge. As Mike and I continued our float down the Gila, amazed that the trickle of water was still deep enough to paddle, I considered how I might help in that effort.

When the packraft trip was over, I drove up into the headwaters of the Gila River in the Gila National Forest. Much of it had burned recently, leaving a haunting wildfire scar—a scene that was becoming more and more common across the West. On my second night, I camped by a spring and watched elk grazing nearby until dark. Suddenly, I heard an explosion of cracking hoofbeats. I realized it was elk running—their hooves pounding over deadfall trees. Something was chasing them.

When the noise died down, I lay down under my rain tarp—then heard something new. The sound got closer. From under my tarp, I saw starlight glinting in one and then two sets of eyes some fifteen yards away. Then I heard panting.

Wolves.

I watched them, on edge, as they circled around me—an unusual behavior, as wolves are quite shy in real life, despite childhood fables that suggest otherwise. Finally, they wandered away and I started to doze off, but their howling, just yards away in the inky blackness, woke me up repeatedly throughout the night. It felt like they were toying with me, knowing it was far too dark for my camera to capture their elusive image.

The next morning, wolf tracks circled my tarp and sleeping bag. They'd taken an interest in my spot and my food, but didn't take or eat anything and never came very close to me. It felt more like a spiritual evening with these keystone species, but also a reminder that wild ecosystems and the remaining wildlife within them are another integral voice that is rarely heard in the fight for rivers and protected lands.

In the Grand Canyon, I'd learned about the power of Native voices, the preciousness of clean, drinkable water, and the ways that silence is an overlooked, underrated gift of our shared wild places. On the Gila, I learned the power of belonging. Simon was right: Conservation couldn't be accomplished by outsiders exclusively—especially if it disproportionately benefited those outsiders while requiring sacrifices from those who called the place home. Conservation movements ought to be spearheaded by the people who know their rivers like family, not by people who swoop in from the city with big cameras and expensive outdoor gear, no matter how well-meaning they might be. And conservation efforts should include the science, biology, and data that support wildlife too—something that's often overlooked.

Standing on the riverbank deflating my packraft, I realized that my relationship with rivers had changed yet again. I'd started out as an adventure photographer chasing the next adrenaline rush. The Colorado had transformed me into a documenter of loss—a witness to all that we were breaking. Now, the Gila was reminding me that maybe my voice wasn't so important after all. My work as a photographer and filmmaker had given me a microphone, but maybe the best thing I could do was hand that microphone to people like Simon Sotelo, Renae Yellowhorse, Carletta Tilousi, and others whose lives were deeply entwined with the places I was traveling through.

Meeting Simon also made me yearn to build a sense of home. Back in Basalt, I found myself gazing around my empty house, wondering what it would be like to really make a life here, instead of using it as a pit stop between assignments. A few weeks later, when Heidi was on the East Coast, I called her.

"Why don't you move out here?" I said. "That way, even if I still travel for work, we can have a home base. We can get a dog. We can live like a normal couple and build memories together."

I didn't realize how much I wanted those things until I said them out loud. My whole adult life, with all the relationships I'd been in, I'd never fully cohabitated with a partner—never shopped for groceries with someone regularly, decorated a shared space, or taken turns watering the same garden. Never gone on a speaking tour or a magazine assignment knowing that someone I loved would be there when I got home. As COVID-19 restrictions were beginning to ease I was starting to travel again, but that would mean a different thing when Heidi and I had a baseline of togetherness than it had when we lived in different states. I had recently turned fifty, and I knew that a love like the one I shared with Heidi was scarcer than water in the remote alcoves of the Grand Canyon. I would do whatever it took to keep it alive.

Chapter 10

What Rises from the Depths

Even after Heidi agreed to move to Colorado, it would still be a few months before she could wrap up her work on the East Coast, finish the lease on her apartment, and find a new job out west.

I distracted myself from the agony of waiting by spending time at my parents' place, interviewing them about the challenges and subtle wonders of aging. I'd decided I needed to do more to document them and their contagious joie de vivre. I'd never met anyone quite like them, and I wanted to mine their wisdom while I still had the chance.

One day, I stood with my mom near the grass runway and watched my dad land the Cub a little more bouncily than he used to.

"How long are you going to keep flying?" I asked him when he emerged from the cockpit, his cap a little askew. He was walking with a bit of a wobble these days, his back hunched forward as if he could tumble down face-first at any time.

"Until I crash," he said.

"Well, try not to do *that*," I laughed. I remembered what my mom had said about him being in denial about his slower glide path. When he became unsafe to fly, would he realize it? And if he realized it, would he admit it? Or would he doggedly insist that nothing had changed, the same way some people insist that the climate isn't changing in the face of extreme weather and abundant scientific evidence? I turned to my mom. "What do you think about your eighty-three-year-old husband flying?" I said.

"Well, he's safer in a plane than he is in a car," she said wearily. My dad piped up. "Or in a bed!"

I found it reassuring that my dad was still cracking himself up—it meant he was still himself, still holding on to some aspects of his identity. Even his mild defensiveness about the plane felt strangely comforting to me. He wasn't going to stop living fully a single millisecond sooner than he had to.

≈

That summer, I took an assignment for *National Geographic* to float the Yampa River in northwestern Colorado on the tail end of its high water run. I invited my friend Len Necefer, whom I'd met recently at a film festival in Telluride, and who shared an interest in our changing natural world. Len had a PhD but had given up his office job to become a filmmaker and storyteller and become a voice for the voiceless. As a member of the Navajo Nation, Len had grown up keenly aware of the injustices that have gone hand in hand with the conservation movement over time. As Len reminded me, it's all too often the colonizers who have the time and resources to buy fancy camping equipment and spend their summers outdoors—not the colonized.

Len and I decided to travel the last fifty miles of the Yampa through Dinosaur National Monument, to see how even a wild river inside a national park was struggling to stay wet during an extreme drought. The 250-mile-long Yampa is one of the only free-flowing rivers in the western United States, and the longest free-flowing river in Colorado. Was it faring any better than the tributaries with dams?

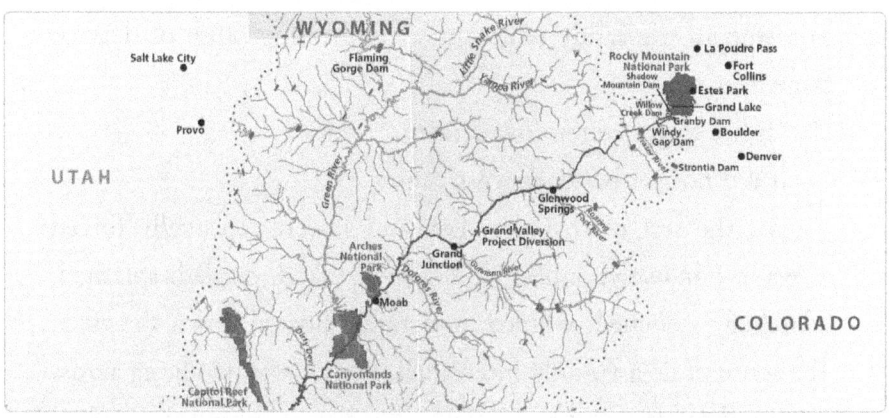

The Yampa River originates near Rocky Mountain National Park in northwest Colorado and flows west before joining the Green River near the Colorado–Utah border.

For weeks before we left, I monitored stream flow gauges, wondering if we might see the river dry up entirely. On August 18, the hydrological curve of the Yampa at Deerlodge Park, where we planned to put in, plummeted to 45 cubic feet per second (cfs)—one of the lowest levels in recorded history. According to US Geological Survey data, the average flow on that day over the last thirty-six years was 330 cfs. I warned Len to pack as lightly as possible and be prepared to walk.

On the morning of August 20, after Len sang a Navajo prayer and gave a small cornmeal offering for the river and our safe passage, we shoved off. That morning, the river gauge doubled to 70 cfs. Either some rain nearby was helping, or ranchers upstream had shut off irrigation ditches to cut hay. Or maybe someone was listening to Len's prayer. Whatever its source, the surge added an inch of floatable depth to the ankle-deep ripples before us.

But just a quarter mile from our put in, the river channel braided, the water thinned, and our little rubber boats screeched to a stop in the sandy sediment. A nauseating sense of déjà vu came over me.

"It has to get better downstream," I said.

It did not get better downstream.

For the rest of that day, Len and I were repeatedly forced to walk. For twelve miles, we dragged, hiked, carried, splashed, scratched, scooched, whined, and rarely floated down the river. The sense of déjà vu only intensified. Here I was, trudging across yet another dry riverbed—only this time, that dry riverbed belonged to a wild, free-flowing, "protected" river.

I felt a creeping numbness. Was this simply the new normal? In fifty years, would people even remember a time when paddling trips in the West didn't mostly consist of sweaty portages? Would we be taking selfies beside ankle-deep water, excited to tell our friends that we'd managed to float or paddle *some* of the time?

I glanced at Len, watching his face as he took in the parched landscape. The dismay in his expression reminded me that this wasn't normal, and we shouldn't allow ourselves to accept it as such.

I knew that the Yampa represented an environmental victory, albeit an imperfect one. In the 1950s, the Yampa became the center of a national fight in Washington, DC, when the US Bureau of Reclamation proposed a dam just below the confluence of the Green River and the Yampa River within Dinosaur National Monument.

If completed, the Echo Park Dam would have flooded much of the Green and the lower Yampa that Len and I had just traveled, including archaeological sites and pictographs. Conservationists opposed the project on the grounds that it encroached into the national monument. After much national debate, the project was abandoned in 1955—in favor of Glen Canyon Dam.

It seemed crazy to me that the government would agree to save the Yampa and then turn around and flood Glen Canyon instead. Surely they were equivalent in ecological and cultural significance. Yet the Echo Park Dam would have fallen within a national monument—a place we had *officially* recognized as being worthy of protection. This gave conservationists ammunition when it came to pushing back against the dam; indeed, the case led to the passage of the Colorado River Storage Project of 1956, which prohibited dams in national parks and monuments.

What we didn't fully understand back then is that wild rivers historically ran dry and flooded in natural cycles, and species like the humpback chub evolved around that hydrologic curve. The Yampa still has that wild variability, but now with much less water overall. What passes for a "flood" today might have been simply a normal flow a hundred years ago; the river is drying up sooner and staying dry longer. Despite having no major dams, there are still plenty of straws in the Yampa's proverbial soda cup—meaning even this somewhat "protected" river is still at risk.

Fifty miles later, Len and I reached our destination: the confluence of the Green River. As we packed up our gear and drove home, we reflected on how differently the Yampa paddle had gone than expected. We made plans to return in a few years to document (and hopefully float) a wetter river.

After the trip, I interviewed some of the angels that help keep the Yampa itself flowing. Jojo La, an endangered species specialist, provided the last line of defense for the river's four endangered fish: the humpback and bonytail chub, the pikeminnow, and the razorback sucker. When the flow gauges plummet toward zero, the Colorado Department of Natural Resources releases pulses of Colorado-owned water from Elkhead Reservoir to keep these fish alive. A few days before our trip ended, it turned out, La's team had conducted a controlled release intended to keep the river alive. Without it, Len and I most likely would have been forced to walk the entire way.

The irony wasn't lost on me: Here was a "wild" river that now depended on engineering from humans to survive. We'd protected the Yampa from dams, but we couldn't protect it from drought and overuse—even as a free-flowing river, much of its water is still diverted for use upstream. Without constant vigilance, we would lose this protected river just the same as we were losing the Colorado.

When I got back from the Yampa trip, I became more and more determined to document my dad's stories and memories. I shot little clips of him imitating birds chirping in the yard, or lip-syncing along to opera while a fire roared in the woodstove nearby. I set up a projector and showed him old film reels from when he and my mom were younger. One clip shows him bounding down a big white sand dune in giant leaps, then executing a perfect dive into a lake. In another, he's exploring a landscape of sandstone alcoves, natural bridges, and smooth-walled slot canyons.

"Dad," I said, "is that Glen Canyon?"

"Oh yes," he said. "I took a trip there with some friends in 1968. They'd started flooding it in 1963, but it took years to fill up all the way."

"You're so lucky you got to see it," I said. "You know, some people say it was even more beautiful than the Grand Canyon."

"They might be right," he said.

He fell silent, and we watched the flickering images, hypnotized by a world that had been lost forever.

"Dad," I said, "remember when you took us all on vacation to Lake Powell? I must have been six or seven on our first trip there. Weren't you upset about Glen Canyon being gone? Lots of people didn't realize what we destroyed to build Lake Powell, but you did."

I thought about how we'd spend whole days cruising the reservoir's twisting channels, the spray cooling our faces as we skimmed across the water in a boat or on water skis. I remembered my dad telling us about the sunken forests far below, but I couldn't remember him expressing outrage or sadness about it.

He paused, as if racking his brain for an answer. "You kids were so happy out there on the lake, learning to water-ski, splashing around. Sometimes it's easier to focus on the positive than to think about all you've lost."

Later that night, I rewatched the Glen Canyon clips alone at my house in Basalt and paged through my dad's old copy of Bruce Berger's book *There Was a River: Essays on the Southwest*. Berger was one of the last people to float through Glen Canyon before it was flooded. He wrote,

> One by one the sand bars, the river banks, the hidden oases of the side canyons succumbed. And with them died all they supported—the cottonwoods, willows, redbuds. . . . Torn from all that sustained them, the herons and egrets had nowhere to go. Ruins, petroglyphs, pictographs, dredges, history disappeared.

Looking at the grainy frames of my dad's footage, I saw a glimpse of what Berger and others were mourning. When my dad visited in 1968 with Berger, there were still plenty of marvels that hadn't yet been submerged. Cottonwood groves flourished along the riverbanks. Natural bridges spanned side canyons. Indigenous cliff dwellings were tucked into sheltered alcoves. And everywhere was the golden-green shimmer of life sustained by a river that still had the appearance of being free-flowing, even though its death sentence had already been written and signed.

Dad appeared in several shots—lean, sunburned, his movements fluid and confident. He scrambled up slickrock slopes, gestured toward arches, and waded in reflective pools. On film, his face shows only the joy of being outdoors on an adventure. But I could tell he felt moments of distress at seeing natural and archeological wonders for the last time, too. He focused much of his limited Super 8 film stock on slowly panning across ancient rock art on the walls as he and his friends explored. I wondered what heartbreak and bewilderment they experienced knowing that what they were witnessing would soon be flooded and—as far as anyone knew—lost forever.

Lately, I'd been seeing dire news headlines about Lake Powell. As of July, the water level in the reservoir had dropped to its lowest point since 1969. By September, the reservoir was at 30 percent capacity—in other words, it was 70 percent empty. If it dropped much lower, it would reach minimum power pool: the threshold beyond which there is no longer enough water to turn the massive turbines in the dam to generate electricity. If the lake level dropped 120 feet lower, it would reach the dreaded "dead pool," when the water level is too low to pass through the dam's lowest outlets, stopping all flow downstream of the reservoir—a possibility that keeps dam operators awake at night. For reference, full pool is 3,700 feet above sea level (Bureau of Reclamation speak), so the lake had already dropped over 260 feet and was still shrinking.

If Lake Powell ever reaches dead pool, it will mean that the main stem of the Colorado River will simply stop flowing upstream of the Grand Canyon, forcing us to drill bypass tunnels lower than the current intakes in Lake Powell—not just to keep the river flowing, but to fulfill all the water demands downstream. And since the water levels in Lake Powell, America's second-largest reservoir, are managed in conjunction with Lake Mead, America's largest reservoir, their water levels often mirror each other year to year. So dead pool in Powell means it could be looming in Mead's future too.

The possibility of dead pool, even if temporary, is apocalyptic to contemplate: No hydroelectric power for millions of people;

a pause on irrigation for millions of acres of crops; severe habitat loss for threatened and endangered species of fish; and a very different rafting line through Lava Falls, one with exposed rocks everywhere. Until bypass tunnels were drilled, the Grand Canyon would contain only thin, ephemeral flows from tributaries downstream; the boating world would wither or halt, and the plants and animals would suffer. Meanwhile, the water trapped in Lake Powell would soon turn into a warm soup of piled-up sediment and algal blooms that not even the most intrepid house boater would want to explore. These are just a few of the abrupt changes we'd witness if this southwest lifeline ceased. Many more impacts would ripple across the West.

In order to avoid this dire fate, water managers took emergency measures to raise the water level in Lake Powell. They ordered the release of water from other reservoirs upstream, and took the almost unheard-of step of imposing water cutbacks on a handful of states. Meanwhile, hotter temperatures meant that any water being released into Lake Powell was also evaporating at a faster rate. I wondered what the engineers who designed the Glen Canyon Dam would think if they could see Lake Powell now, not even sixty years later. Would they still believe they'd harnessed the power of nature toward a wise end? Would some still believe the old adage that "rain follows the plow"?

There was one paradoxical upside to this slow-motion disaster: Parts of Glen Canyon that had been underwater since before my birth were emerging from the depths. Maybe some of the marvels my dad and his friends had seen would know the sun again, if only for a short time. It occurred to me that it might be possible to see some of the same places that my father had filmed half a century ago—and once that thought was in my mind, I couldn't let it go.

~

The next morning, I called up Len and asked if he'd like to visit Lake Powell with me that spring.

He immediately understood the significance of this journey.

"Let's go see what's rising from the reservoir," he said.

Come April, Len and I found ourselves in a ghost forest in what was once Lake Powell, along with our friend Eric Balken from the Glen Canyon Institute. Dead cottonwoods towered around us, their blackened trunks encrusted with white mineral deposits. For decades, these trees had stood submerged in hundreds of feet of water, preserved rather than decomposed in the cold depths. The base of each trunk was swallowed by fine-grained silt that matched the surrounding sandstone.

I felt a complicated hope. On the one hand, I wanted to cheer for those cottonwood trees whose dead branches got to touch the sun in defiance of the engineers' plans to submerge them forever. I imagined new trees growing up from the silt, replacing the forest that was lost; I imagined the beavers coming back, the bonytail chub and pikeminnow rebounding. On the other hand, I didn't want the reason for this extraordinary comeback to be a catastrophic drought that would have devastating consequences for other places I cared about. I wanted Glen Canyon to return because we'd joined together to rescue it, not because the situation had become so dire that our entire western plumbing system was falling apart.

A mineralized cottonwood tree rises from the floor of Glen Canyon, exposed by falling water levels.

"Wild," Len said, observing the newly exposed lake floor. "The canyon is returning. Nature bats last."

"I guess so," I replied. "Especially when you're playing with deep, geologic time."

The contradiction pulled at me. Here I was, celebrating the resurrection of a place while simultaneously dreading what its reappearance signified for the region's water supply. This was a glimpse into our future—learning to find moments of wonder and complicated beauty in landscapes radically altered by climate change.

We were walking in almost exactly the same locations my father had filmed in 1968. Lines of cement-colored sediment—the "bathtub ring" marking high water—encircled the sandstone walls around us. On the canyon floor, partially buried recreation detritus—beer cans, golf balls, lawn chairs, even a sunken Jet Ski—created a bizarre time capsule of recent human presence amid ancient stone. I wondered what Bruce Berger would think if he could see this strange archeological record of the lake that had drowned his beloved canyon.

It struck me how the river and my father had mirrored each other throughout his lifetime. Once, both had been wild and vibrant, flowing with seemingly limitless energy. Now both had been fundamentally altered—my father by the claws of age and time, the river by dams and diversions. Both still existed, but in forms that were increasingly constrained, their essential nature changed.

My dad's decline, though heartbreaking, was part of the natural cycle of human life. But what we had done to the Colorado River was different—an attempt to control a natural phenomenon for our own benefit, putting human desires first while ignoring the winged, finned, and clawed creatures who also depended on this water. If we had taken other species into account, the way Native peoples had been doing for millennia, we never would have gotten into this jam in the first place. I knew that when my dad passed away, my grief for him would be fierce and intense. But losing a parent is normal and natural; there are rituals and cultural scripts to ease the passage. What cultural scripts do we have to grieve the death of a river?

As Len and I ventured deeper into side canyons, we discovered something unexpected: life returning. Hidden in a drainage, freshwater desert orchids bloomed along seeps that had been flooded for most of my lifetime and only recently been exposed. "I didn't expect to see orchids returning so quickly," Eric said, excitement in his voice. "It almost feels wild again."

In one alcove known as Cathedral in the Desert, a waterfall trickled through a gap in an overhang hundreds of feet above. Further along, Len and I encountered Gregory Natural Bridge, a 137-foot sandstone arch that had been submerged since the dam's completion. That summer, boats would motor beneath it for the first time in generations.

There was a hard truth staring me in the face: All decline involves loss, but not all loss is equal. My father's aging followed the natural trajectory of a human lifespan. But what we've done to the Colorado River represents something different—an unnatural and unnecessary death driven by short-term thinking and the profit motive.

At one point, Eric, Len, and I found the exact spot where my father had stood and filmed rock art and ancient dwellings. Now, it was almost all gone, washed away by the water. Len was visibly shaken by the level of destruction the man-made lake had wrought.

"It's sad to see your dad's footage, then come here and see that there are just foundations left. It looks like a bomb went off and blew these houses to smithereens," he said.

He gestured to the scum on the walls of the canyon, layers of built-up calcium obscuring the rock art. "When we talk about the erasure of Native history, it's often a metaphor—but here, the erasure is literal. It's incredibly frustrating. What other place in the world would we allow this to happen and not even talk about it?"

Eric Balken and Len Necefer hike through Glen Canyon. The rings of buildup on the canyon walls mark previous high water lines.

I felt the heat of Len's anger. The casual destruction of Native art and artifacts speaks volumes about our country's history. Yet, ambling around Glen Canyon, I also found moments of unexpected hope. If the orchids could return after decades underwater, what other forms of regeneration might still be possible?

As the light faded, I packed my camera and prepared to leave. Tomorrow we would document more resurrections. For now, it was enough to stand in a canyon my father had explored half a century ago and feel how small I was in the vastness of time.

When I got home, my dad and I drove down one of the old dirt roads crisscrossing the ranch and took a short hike to check out a drainage.

"This has *never* been dry at this time of year," he said, leaning heavily on his hiking poles. "It's always full, half full. Can you believe it?"

"It's aridification," I said, remembering the conversation Mike and I had on the Gila. "We're living in a whole different climate from when you guys bought this place in '79."

As I followed my dad back to the truck, I asked him a question. "Dad, what are you most proud of? The conservation easement? The affordable housing you built? The junior hockey program you started?"

Ever since the COVID pandemic, I'd had a lot of time to think about my own legacy—the traces I wanted to leave behind, whether or not I had kids. It seemed to me that my dad had done everything he'd ever set out to do: he'd raised a family, built community in Aspen, traveled the world, supported the causes he valued, and protected an amazing piece of land in perpetuity. Of course, he'd come of age at a time when all those things were a lot simpler than they are today, but I still looked to him as a model of a life well-lived.

"No one thing," he replied, his hiking poles poking the ground. "I've been lucky. I've had a good life, doing things I believed in."

I thought this rather vague reply was the whole of his answer. Then he stopped walking and wheeled around to face me, his eyes brightening. "Actually, you know what? One of the things I'm most proud of . . . is *you*." He jabbed his finger toward me.

"You've done so many wonderful things. You're so dedicated to good causes. You have a focus that's so important."

He grinned broadly, like he'd just revealed a surprise he'd been waiting to give me for years. Gone was the stern hockey coach shouting at me to skate harder, and the stressed-out businessman struggling to downshift for a family vacation. Now, all I saw in his face was pure love. It was like aging had caused him to forget all the reasons he used to have for hiding his affection—ideas about toughness and self-reliance.

Now, I saw that life had softened him like a river current polishing and smoothing the stones of its bed. The claws of aging take away, but they also reveal something new. In an instant, all the self-doubt I'd had about the value of my work, the grouchiness I felt about giving the same talks over and over, and the questions I'd been asking myself about whether or not I was making an impact fell away. My dad was proud of me—and knowing what a discerning person he is, that meant there must be something there to be proud of.

"I'm proud of all of you kids. And you know what?" he added as I hurried to wipe away a tear. "That girl Heidi is a gem—a real keeper. I'm so glad you found someone who can keep up with you—and someone worth slowing down for."

After a pause, he returned to his usual tough-love humor. "Of course, I have no idea what she sees in you. You are way too old for her, so don't screw it up."

A few weeks later, I stood beside my dad in the hayfield, watching him go through his preflight checklist on the Cub.

"Dad, we really need to pull more of these dead mice out of here," I told him, gesturing toward the fabric-covered wing where hundreds of rodents had been nesting all winter, having snuck in through the tail wheel and crawled up the fuselage.

He waved me off with a chuckle. "Ah, they're fine. A few mice never hurt anybody."

As I watched him work through his safety checks, I noticed he was skipping things. He did a thorough fuel test, but when he got to the control surfaces he only gave the elevator a half-hearted wiggle. I started filming him, training my lens on his hands.

"Oil level?" I asked, knowing he sometimes forgot that one.

"Checked it," he said. But I hadn't seen him lift the cowling.

Before we took off, I noticed the airspeed protective cover was still on. It has a big red flag on it for this exact reason, as it's easy to forget.

"Dad—hold up. The airspeed cover's still on. Hold the brakes."

"Oh, look at that. Good catch. Be careful of the prop," he said.

I climbed out of the back seat and ran around to the other wing to remove the small Velcro-strapped sleeve. Then I crawled my way into the back from behind the wing strut, all while the engine idled, the prop spinning.

"Good show, Peto," said my dad. "All buckled up?"

"Yep," I replied.

Inside the cockpit, my dad seemed distracted as he flipped the light switches and tapped the oil temp gauge. He reminded me of his favorite C.I.G.A.R. T.I.P. checklist, and we ran through it together: controls, instruments, gas, altimeter, radios, trim, interior, prop. We settled into our seats, and he did a clean takeoff from the bumpy little strip in the hayfield in front of the house.

"Ratatouille Airlines, this is your copilot speaking," I joked through my headset. "We have a *very* full flight today, with approximately two hundred furry passengers. However, the captain has asked me to inform you that snack service in the wings has been suspended indefinitely."

"Everyone needs to go somewhere at some point . . ." my father joked back on the intercom. As we rose into the air, the beauty of the valley revealed itself from a thousand feet above the runway. When I thought of all the times we'd flown together, I felt a soreness in my throat and choked back a wave of emotion. Although I'd been reluctant to admit it, I think I knew this would be the last flight I would ever take with my dad in the pilot seat.

For years now, I'd been documenting endings: the last time the Colorado River kissed the sea; the last mile you could walk or raft through the Grand Canyon before the drone of helicopters shattered the silence; the last time our mountain creeks flowed at full capacity. None of those endings, as heart-wrenching as they were, had prepared me for the flood of emotion I felt as I watched my dad's hands on the stick, knowing this would be the last time he controlled it.

I opened the side window and reached my arm into the seventy-five-mile-per-hour wind, gripping my camera tightly to film my father flying from the seat in front of me. I wanted to get a few frames of him in his favorite spot, a pilot in command of his aerial perch.

When I was finished shooting, I retracted my arm, chilled by the wind, and closed the window.

"You know, I'm pretty close to getting my pilot's license," I said. "Maybe you should think about selling me this Cub. I'll keep Ratatouille Airlines airborne for you. And then one day, I'll take you flying."

"That's great, Peto," he said. "Get your license and another Cub so we can fly together in formation."

He chuckled, but then grew serious. "As you know, owning a plane is a lot of responsibility," he said. "You need to maintain it. Keep it registered. Get your biennial flight reviews. Fill out your logs. And you have to fly regularly to stay safe. You can't dart off on assignments all the time."

"I know. I'm committed to doing it right."

"And always fly in calm weather. I always fly in the mornings. They're the best, with good calm air."

He sounded like exactly what he was: a parent instructing a child. A parent I trusted, instructing a child *he* trusted to take up where he had left off.

As we flew up the Fryingpan River valley, low and slow, he asked, "You want to take the controls for a bit?"

"Sure," I said.

I grabbed the stick with my right hand and put my left on the throttle, then placed my feet on the rudder pedals. "My controls," I said, confirming I had taken over as pilot, then wiggled the wings with the stick and rudder inputs. As we flew up the river toward Ruedi Reservoir, I kept us smooth and coordinated, and listened for any jet traffic crossing above us.

We kept chatting through the static of our headsets, like we had for decades, about the landscape below, the low water, family, my relationship with Heidi . . . our usual father-and-son pattern.

With the noisy din of the engine, our conversations in the air always went straight to the essentials.

After thirty minutes, I turned us around over the reservoir we had skated on years earlier. Its water level was so low you could see visible bathtub rings. As we headed back to our high-altitude grass runway, he took over the controls again and said, "You flew well. You'll make a great pilot one day."

Conclusion

It was late May. Fuzzy green catkins had just started to appear on the aspen trees, mountain bluebirds were making their nests in abandoned woodpecker holes, and the black bears had emerged from their dens. My brother Johno and I were wrenching on a vehicle when my cell phone began to ring. I glanced down at the caller ID.

"Huh," I said. "I wonder why the water commissioner's calling."

I answered the call and wandered a few feet away to stand in the sun while I talked to the commissioner.

"What was *that* about?" Johno said when I hung up.

"We just got our water called," I said, feeling a little dazed. "They want us to close our ditch before the creek runs dry."

He stared at me. "For real? It's only *May*."

I shrugged. "I know. The water commissioner was just as surprised. He said he's never seen it like this, ever. You've seen how low the creek is, and the snowpack. Or rather, the lack of snowpack."

We went into the house and pulled on thick knee-high boots, then walked across the big pasture filled with lowing black cows to the ditch that had been carrying snowmelt to our ranch for as long as I could remember.

As I wrestled with the heavy apron that diverts water from the creek into our ditch, everything felt surreal. When I was growing up, this creek would have been a raging torrent at this time of year, swollen with snowmelt. You couldn't have stepped into it without a very real danger of getting washed away. Once, when I was a kid, I'd tried to cross the creek on a small ATV, and the flow was so strong it flipped the ATV over. I managed to swim to shore, and the three-wheeler was swept forty yards downstream and got tangled up in a willow. We had a heck of a time extracting it. And I was scared of that creek for years to come.

Now, that same stream was a trickle that barely skimmed my ankles. Seeing the Colorado River run dry in Mexico was bad enough; seeing a tributary run dry near the headwaters in springtime was downright insane.

I hefted the apron aside, and muddy brown water began to flow down into the creek instead of taking a left turn into the ditch. A high-pitched screeching sound rang out as Johno cranked the metal headgate shut one quarter inch at a time.

"Hopefully this is only for a little while," I said. "Maybe things will pick up again in a few weeks and they'll let us open it again."

In the meantime, though, I knew that closing the ditch was the right thing to do. People downstream from us needed that water—and perhaps more important, so did the creek itself.

Within a few minutes of closing the headgate, all that was left in the ditch were a few shallow puddles. Johno leaned over the bank and reached into the water to rescue a fish that had gotten trapped on the wrong side, soaking the sleeves of his gray sweatshirt. Once he had it in his hands—a shimmering, silvery native brook trout about ten inches long—he jogged through the tall grass and deposited it gently in the still-flowing creek on the other side.

"Go on and live, little buddy," I said as he shooed it on its way.

~

A few weeks later, my dad went out to fly on his own. He started the plane and taxied to the end of the runway—then turned around, came back to the hangar, and parked without telling anybody why.

"You still want to buy this plane, Peto?" he asked me the next time I saw him. My mom had told me about his taxi and return. I wondered what had made him change his mind. Maybe something had scared him.

"Of course I do," I said. "I want to take you flying one day."

He gave me a price I couldn't refuse—more than he'd paid, but cheaper than market—and that was that: he hung up his wings. The next week, he handed me a weathered brown folder with the plane's mechanical reports and a mishmash of paperwork for it, as well as some old maps and navigation tools, like a metal E6B with a custom leather case (today they're made of flimsy plastic). I felt grateful that he'd stopped flying on his terms and that an accident hadn't decided the future for us. I hadn't even realized how much I'd been dreading that conversation until I realized we'd never have to have it.

My dad had the wisdom to set his own limits. It's the kind of self-awareness our entire civilization could use more of: the ability to recognize when we've reached the edge of what's sustainable and step back before we crash.

I'd been thinking a lot about that kind of wisdom as I worked on my latest film, a short called *Monumental Moment*. Back in 2022, Carletta Tilousi, as part of a group called the Grand Canyon Tribal Coalition, had formally proposed the designation of a new national monument near the rim of the Grand Canyon. In August 2023, Carletta's teenaged daughter Maya, whom I had met and filmed nearly a decade earlier while protesting uranium mining, had introduced President Biden at the monument's official commemoration ceremony in Red Butte.

The monument's very name—Baaj Nwaavjo I'tah Kukveni – Ancestral Footprints of the Grand Canyon National Monument—honors the Havasupai and Hopi languages and acknowledges that these are Indigenous homelands first and foremost. Baaj Nwaavjo means "where tribes roam" in Havasupai, and I'tah Kukveni means "our ancestral footprints" in Hopi. The naming itself was an act of restoration—a small but significant reclamation of what had been lost.

Although existing uranium mines would still be allowed to operate, no new mining claims would be issued. Like so many environmental victories, this one was bittersweet. Mines like Canyon Mine (now called Pinyon Plain Mine), which stands just three miles from where the ceremony took place, were allowed to continue operating. The Havasupai would continue to fight the existing mines, even as they celebrated the new protections on their sacred land.

Carletta and her family knew the current approach to resource extraction was threatening to crash the ecosystem, and while one administration had listened, the next said it would review the monument and others and possibly reverse directions. It reminded me that each generation needs to decide to stand up for what they want to protect. You only have to lose one fight for something you love to be gone forever, because it's rare for us to undo development once it's done.

~

On a clear July morning, I woke Heidi up early to take her on a hike. She grumbled about the early hour. "Will this really be worth it?" she asked.

"Trust me," I said. "We need to beat the crowds."

She rallied, and an hour later we were hiking some six miles up to a giant granite outcrop on the way to a remote pass above an alpine lake, accompanied by our new rescue dog, Oso. Sitting atop the rock, looking down the drainage from our eleven-thousand-foot-high perch and surrounded by sprays of wild columbine flowers, we shared peanut butter sandwiches—Heidi's favorite.

I told myself, *Well, this is as good a place as any.*

With Heidi on my left and Oso on my right, I got on one knee and pulled out a ring I had made from one of my guitar strings—a string on which I had played many bluegrass and folk song meanderings for Heidi's generous approval.

"I fell in love with you the instant I met you, so . . . " I said, then stuttered and started to get emotional.

"What the hell? I have a mouthful of trail mix. Wait—" she said.

I waited a split second. Once she'd swallowed the rest of her almonds and raisins, I continued.

"I have way more to say, but . . . will you marry me?"

"What the hell?" Heidi echoed herself in surprise. Not sensing an immediate yes, I pulled out a small black velvet box. When I showed her the "real" ring, she put her hands to her mouth in shock. Before I could say or do anything else, Heidi grabbed the ring and tried it on. It fit perfectly.

"*Yeeeeesss*, yes, yes!" she said as tears welled in her eyes. As if on cue, Oso put his paws on her shoulder as we hugged. (He does not like to be left out.)

Afterward, we snapped photos in the columbine corridor, then hiked further up into the headwaters of the Colorado River. The wildflowers had bloomed early due to the drought. Despite the low snowpack, the mountains were sublime. We talked excitedly about ideas for our wedding, and laughed about how I had surprised her, despite a series of hints that she had overlooked.

The next night, we had our regular Sunday family dinner with my siblings and nieces and nephew and parents. I made a short and simple toast to Heidi and her patience and then told everyone we were engaged. They all erupted in surprise. My nephew Jasper hollered in delight, and Riley, my sister's oldest and often the most stoic, teared up.

My father hugged me and said, "You've done good, kid. She's a star. It's about time."

―

Weeks later, on a cool, windless morning, I slowly walked to the edge of a hay meadow with my father beside me, hunched over a bit but moving well. My mother followed right behind.

"Looks like a great day to fly," he said.

"It's gorgeous," said my mother from behind. The old Super Cub sat just ahead of us, parked in the grass. Its wings had been refurbished and their new yellow covering glowed in the morning light. After buying the plane from my father, I had spoken with the mechanic who had cared for it for decades.

"It's time to redo those wings," he'd said. "The mouse house situation is way worse than you realize. There are twenty pounds of acorns in each wing!"

Now, my parents marveled at the improvement.

"Wow, she looks almost new," my dad said.

"Yup—shinier, and lighter too. Now let's see if we can get you in the back seat."

"Do I have to sit back there?" he asked, smirking a bit. "That's *your* seat."

"I know, but I can't control the flaps or radios from back there," I grinned back. "Don't worry, it's not that bad—I only threw up back there once, and that was forty years ago."

"Come on, Tumpi, get in there," my mother chimed in, calling him by the same endearing nickname she'd used since they first met. I still have no idea what it means or how it came to be.

After some arm-holding and gently trying to thread one leg around the control stick, we concluded that my father's artificial hips and octogenarian knees were a bit too stiff to get into the cramped back seat. Pulling his full body weight over the drop-down door entry also proved tricky.

"I'm sorry, boy, I don't think I can get in."

"Let me figure out a way, Pabo. I can pull the front seat out."

"No, don't worry. I've done my flying. I actually just like watching you."

Not ready to give up on my dream of taking him flying, I looked at him and said, "I'll get you up soon and give you my camera, Pabo."

"No, you keep the camera. That's still your role," he replied. "We need you to keep reminding everyone about water—and the wonder in the world."

Sensing a shift in the cycles of life, I walked my father to an old wicker chair by a fence post overlooking the field and thanked him for giving me wings for so many years. He told me how delighted he was to see me fix up and fly his favorite plane.

"Now go fly—fly safely," he said, smiling.

"I will. Love you."

And with that, I trotted to the plane, climbed in, put the seat belt harness on, hollered "Clear!" and started the engine. Its two-blade propeller jumped to life and I taxied to the top of the runway, bumping over gopher holes. After turning, I went through the flight checklist my father had engrained into me during my training and then pushed the throttle open.

The 1978 Super Cub rumbled to life and bounded downhill along the same runway where I'd sat behind my father for roughly four decades. Now in his seat, alone, I lifted off and dipped the left wing down and up, an aviation nod of sorts, as I zoomed past him at 60 miles per hour ten feet above the hay meadow. He gave me a steady wave as I went by.

I climbed a few hundred feet and followed the silver ribbon of life, the creek that supplies everyone's irrigation ditches in the area. Despite enduring one of the driest summers in recorded history, the waterway still glimmered as it wove its way north toward the Roaring Fork River. From there, its water would join the Colorado

River 45 miles to the west—flowing toward our hopes, our needs, and our seemingly endless thirst downstream.

While I don't know if my father will ever be able to fly with me again, one thing is certain: I will keep my gaze wide, documenting the fragile beauty around us in the time we have left. My focus remains on that simple yet indispensable resource—and on the beautiful, fragile artery that carries it—the Colorado River.

Whether or not we can sustain this river will depend on our willingness to overcome apathy and fight indifference, and on our capacity to remember that we're not the only ones who need water. We're borrowing something that belongs to an entire ecosystem, rather than claiming something that is ours alone.

Fresh water belongs to the mountain peaks, the quiet streams, and the flooding rivers; it belongs to the forests and deltas; it belongs to our wild friends the elk, black bear, mountain lion, osprey, pikeminnow, wood frog, tarantula hawk, and tarantula just as much as it does to our engineered municipal and agricultural needs.

When we allocate more attention to these other forms of life, we learn the profound lesson of coexistence. In doing so, we may quench our deepest thirst: not by taking more water, but by asking for less—and in that restraint, discover what makes us truly human.

Afterword

Dragging the packraft across the rocks in the heat was brutal. The Yampa River was so low we had no choice but to haul our boats through shallow, cobbled stretches, sweating under the sun, trying to make progress inch by inch. At one point, we stopped and considered our options. We could pack everything on our backs and walk the banks, which would be nearly twice as fast—but that meant rattlesnakes, unrelenting heat, and no way to cool off. Or we could stay in the shallow water, dragging slowly over rocks, conserving our bodies but sacrificing speed. Neither option was good, but we had to choose. We chose the river, knowing that although it was slower, it was sustainable.

That moment has stayed with me, because it felt like a metaphor for the choices we face on the Colorado River. Policy, academia, and lived experience all tell us the same thing: sometimes the future offers only hard trade-offs. And the question becomes: what do we value most? In that moment on the river, survival meant staying cool, even if it also meant grinding slowly downstream. In this basin, survival requires making choices that feel uncomfortable but allow us to keep moving forward.

I wouldn't have been on the Yampa that day if not for my friendship with Pete McBride. Pete has been immersed in the story of this river for decades, documenting and telling its story with unmatched commitment. I came to it through a different path than he did, but what bound us together was a shared love of being outside and a commitment to staying curious, even in a time of immense change and creeping cynicism. Our friendship put me on the river, and it changed the way I saw my own work and future.

When I looked down at that thin trickle of water, I couldn't escape the thought that this was *my* water. If it didn't evaporate in a reservoir downstream, some of it might eventually flow into the Central Arizona Project, through the canals, and come out of my tap in Tucson. The realization that what I was dragging a boat through might someday become what I drank forced me to confront the precarity of our future. And it struck me how few people in Tucson know where their water comes from. Just as few people in the Upper Basin know how proactive Tucson has been in conserving water. Tucson recycles water, restricts grass lawns, and ultimately uses less water per person today than it did decades ago, even while continuing to grow. That disconnect, between upstream and downstream, between policy and lived experience, is one of the great challenges of this river.

I've seen similar dynamics in Native communities. Decisions about our lands and waters are often made by people who don't know our communities or the places we're connected to. It's not always malicious—often it's the result of incentive structures and blind spots—but the distance can still lead to bad policy. On the Colorado River, many decision-makers are working from conference rooms, under pressure to respond to spreadsheets and deadlines, with little chance to see the river for themselves. No chart can capture what it feels like to drag a boat over rocks in the blazing sun. That's why I believe that decision-makers at every level would benefit from spending time on the river: to complement the data with lived experience, to feel scarcity in their bones, and to let that inform the choices ahead.

This is where Pete became my teacher. I sometimes joke that I was doing a postdoc under his leadership. He has been on the river for decades, listening to it in a way no journal article could capture. In turn, I share the tools I carried from my background in policy and research. The back-and-forth between us has been as important as the miles we've traveled. It reminds me that true learning doesn't just happen in classrooms, but in friendship, in shared hardship, and in conversations at the edge of the river.

Academia gave me the skills to parse complexity, to understand the legal and technical scaffolding of water policy. But dragging boats taught me something different: humility, patience, and the weight of lived reality. Each way of knowing enriches the other. Without academic rigor, we risk missing the complexity. Without lived experience, we risk missing the humanity. Both sides need humility.

And now, we are staring down 2026: the big renegotiation year for the Colorado River. According to Jennifer Pitt, Colorado River Program Director at the National Audubon Society, many nonprofits and scientists agree that we should be preparing for shortages of up to four million acre-feet. That number might sound abstract, but it's not. It represents farms, food, cities, energy, and entire ecosystems. It's life in the Southwest. It's daunting, but it's also an opportunity. Crises should be faced head-on. They are openings where entrenched systems can change quickly. We can choose to use these shortages as a reason to retreat, to fight basin against basin. Or we can see them as a chance to change the way we use water—to give more back to nature, to better support agriculture, to design policy that matches the river we have instead of the river we wish we had.

The only way forward is connection between upstream and downstream, between academics and storytellers, between policymakers and people on the ground. We need to invest not just in science but in the connective tissue: storytellers, educators, and bridge-builders. People who can help farmers in the north understand what it's like to live in a desert city, and help people in cities understand the challenges of growing food under shrinking water allotments. Without empathy across the basin, we will fail.

In my friendship with Pete I've found different generations, different starting points, and different languages of expertise, all ultimately bound by a shared love of this river and a refusal to give up. It has taught me that curiosity is an antidote to despair, and that the future of the Colorado River will depend on that same spirit working across boundaries, listening across generations, and staying open to learning from one another.

Human decisions got us here, and human decisions can get us out. The river is not an unsolvable problem. This is not the end of the story. The future is not written. We have an opportunity to write a new chapter: one where the Colorado River continues to sustain us not through illusions of endless supply, but through humility, collaboration, and creativity.

The river teaches us this simple truth—we only get downstream together.

—Len Necefer, PhD

Acknowledgments

During the many decades I've traced, trailed, and trekked the Colorado River, quite often chasing its diminishing water, there has been a constant flow of people who have helped inspire me to keep moving up- and downstream, all generously sharing their wisdom and expertise. I am grateful to scores of experts, from the river rats who master the oars and the mountain goats who thrive in the headwaters' thin air to the many advocates—Native, environmental, scientific, agricultural, legal, and adventurous—who speak up for equity among all river users, including the wild ones without voices.

While there are too many to mention, here are a few who have been instrumental in paddling this book downstream.

To Hilary—thanks for weaving the yarn of thread that landed on your remote shores. Randy and Hierophant, I appreciate the perseverance. This project evolved to exactly where it should be.

To Kevin Fedarko, my trailless hermano, thank you for the generosity of your wisdom and words.

Len Necefer and Eric Balken—to more riparian restorations and nature-batting-last moments ahead. Len, thanks for the big bear perspectives. Jon Waterman—so much of this started with delta dance. Thanks for your wilderness voice.

To Jake Norton and Dave Morton—our Himalaya and Ma Ganga days remain forever sacred.

To the delta paddle team, Juan Butron, Sam Walton, Fred Philips, Osvel Hinojosa, and Rowan Jacobsen—I will always cherish our epic bushwhacking journey and the songs and dances of that rio con agua.

To Carletta, Maya, and the Tilousi family, Renae Yellowhorse, Rita Bilagody, Sarana Riggs, and the Save the Confluence team—thanks for letting me into your world and allowing me to tell your stories.

Harlan Taney, Justin Clifton, Blake McCord, Scott Perry, Oars Rafting, and the Dory crew all carried loads of hospitality on this front, which were greatly appreciated. Jeanne-Philippe Clark, I am still grateful for the rescue. Drs. Sayfie, John Tveten, and Tom Myers, thanks for healing my blistered body, rattled heart and tattered spirit.

To Sadie Quarrier, Quentin Nardi, Jim Muschett, Sabine Meyer, Michelle Smith, and Dan Westergren—your editing eyes and friendship through the years continue to be a grateful gift.

To Matt Rice at American Rivers and Mike DeHoff with Returning Rapids—here's to more tributary, confluence, and low-water adventures. To Jack Schmidt, Peter Culp, Taylor Hawes, Jennifer Pitt, Carlos de La Parra, Carlos Fernandez, and Anne Castle—your council on water and conservation over the years has been generous and deeply appreciated.

To Ethan, Darcy, Jim, and the Grand Canyon Trust team and staff—thanks for the Colorado Plateau support and friendship over the years and for bringing Native voices forward.

To nature's air force pilots, Bruce and Janey Gordon at Ecoflight and Will Worthington with LightHawk—my perspective is much wider thanks to your aerial platforms.

There are scores of dust-encrusted Grand Canyon lovers who showed me how to follow lion tracks and ancient routes through the maze of rock and time; I'd still be lost without you. Mathieu Brown, Kelly McGrath, Amy Martin, Mike St. Pierre, Chris Atwood, Dave Nally, and Matt Mallgrave—your energies and hiking passions inspire far from the "trails." Andrew Holycross—I'm still learning the difference between want and need.

Rich Rudow—thanks for the trust, taking us under your canyon wing, and opening the door to your desert world. To many more "Rutrow" moments.

Katie Hake, your quiet support and technical genius make me grateful beyond words. To the memories of fathers. To Kayla Lindquist and the Sony Alpha team—your support keeps me telling stories in all forms. Deb Benson and the Changemaker team—thanks for honing my live story telling skills.

And last but not least, to my family, for whom I carry a mountain of love.

To my nieces Ruby, Riley, Lucy, and Annalisa and my nephew, Jasper—remember to always hug the quiet and chase the awe and wonder. To my sister, Kato—to many flights, dances and littl' bro adventures ahead. To my brother, Johno—may we always celebrate more follies on rivers, mountain tops, and beyond. Thanks for being granite in my world.

To my mother, "Moutie," your creative spark lights my soul. Thanks for being the glue and for inspiring us all, always. And finally, to my father and wingman, "Pabo," thanks for always guiding me toward awe and wonder. Mucho lovo for you both.

Heidi, your sublime support for my wild soul moves me daily. Thanks for being a bright, loving light and the rudder guiding me home. Te adoro.

About the Author

Pete McBride is an award-winning photographer, filmmaker, writer, and speaker known for his powerful storytelling at the intersection of adventure and environmental conservation. Raised in Colorado, McBride has spent over two decades documenting remote corners of the globe, from the peaks of the Himalayas to the depths of the Grand Canyon.

A National Geographic Explorer, Adventurer of the Year, and Sony Artisan of Imagery, McBride has worked in more than 75 countries, combining his skills in photojournalism and filmmaking to spotlight pressing environmental issues, particularly those involving water scarcity, wilderness protection, and climate change.

His 750-mile trek through the length of the Grand Canyon became the basis for the Emmy-nominated documentary *Into the Canyon* and his celebrated book *The Grand Canyon: Between River and Rim*, which won a National Outdoor Book Award.

His later books, *Seeing Silence* and *Chasing Water*, also won national book awards, and his photography and writing have appeared in *National Geographic, Outside, Smithsonian,* and *The New York Times,* among others. He is a frequent speaker at global conferences and conservation events.

To learn more, visit *petemcbride.com*.